If you have a home computer with Internet access you may:
- request an item to be placed on hold.
- renew an item that is not overdue or on hold.
- view titles and due dates checked out on your card.
- view and/or pay your outstanding fines online ($1 & over).

To view your patron record from your home computer click on Patchogue-Medford Library's homepage: **www.pmlib.org**

SEARCHING
FOR A
King

Also by Jeffry R. Halverson

Master Narratives of Islamist Extremism
(with H. L. Goodall Jr. and S. R. Corman)

Theology and Creed in Sunni Islam:
The Muslim Brotherhood, Ash'arism, and Political Sunnism

Related Titles from Potomac Books

Jihad Joe: Americans Who Go to War in the Name of Islam
—J. M. Berger

Radical Islam in America: Salafism's Journey from Arabia to the West
—Chris Heffelfinger

Virtual Caliphate: Exposing the Islamist State on the Internet
—Yaakov Lappin

SEARCHING
FOR A
King

MUSLIM NONVIOLENCE
AND THE FUTURE
OF ISLAM

JEFFRY R. HALVERSON

Potomac Books
Washington, D.C.

Library of Congress Cataloging-in-Publication Data
Halverson, Jeffry R.
  Searching for a King : Muslim nonviolence and the future of Islam / Jeffry R. Halverson.
    p. cm.
  Includes bibliographical references and index.
  ISBN 978-1-61234-469-0 (hardcover : alk. paper)—ISBN 978-1-61234-470-6 (electronic) 1. Nonviolence—Religious aspects—Islam. 2. Jihad. 3. Islam—21st century. I. Title.
  BP190.5.V56H357 2012
  297.5'697—dc23

                                                          2012018889

Printed in the United States of America on acid-free paper that meets the American National Standards Institute Z39-48 Standard.

Potomac Books
22841 Quicksilver Drive
Dulles, Virginia 20166

First Edition
10 9 8 7 6 5 4 3 2 1

To my nephew Nathan

CONTENTS

ACKNOWLEDGMENTS

The research for this book was supported in part by grants from the Institute for Humanities Research at Arizona State University and the Office of Naval Research. I wish to thank my agent, Elizabeth Evans, and my editor, Hilary Claggett, at Potomac Books for believing in this project. I would also like to thank Professor Abdullahi Gallab at Arizona State University for his comments on chapter 6 and Professors Michael Tucker at Fairfield University and Robert C. Gailey at Point Loma Nazarene University for their comments on chapter 9. Finally, my gratitude goes to my family, my friends, especially Matt and Michelle Correa, and my colleagues in the Hugh Downs School of Human Communication at Arizona State University, namely Angela Trethewey, Steve Corman, Scott Ruston, Chris Lundry, and the rest of the team, for their support and encouragement throughout the research and writing process.

INTRODUCTION

Ten years ago I sat with my back against a concrete pillar and my legs crossed on an old green carpet in a mosque called Masjid ar-Rahman in downtown Cairo. I was a graduate student studying Islam in Egypt as a Fulbright scholar. Across from me sat a well-dressed, clean-shaven Egyptian businessman in his twenties. Martyrdom in jihad, he told me, earns the believers the grace of Allah and opens the gates of paradise to even the most fallible. It sounded much like a sales pitch. He was selling me on the idea of dying in jihad, specifically a military jihad—a crude and narrow understanding of an ancient Islamic concept. I responded politely by quoting a hadith, a recorded saying of the Prophet Muhammad: "The ink of the scholar's pen is holier than the blood of a martyr."

We were conversing in English, which he spoke perfectly, but he did not understand what I meant by the word "holier." I explained as best I could, and finally he understood. It shook him. He paused for a moment, speechless, and asked me about the authenticity of the hadith. Reluctantly, he conceded that the hadith might mean that a scholar could bring others into Islam (i.e., through *dawa*, or propagation), and doing so was certainly commendable—possibly even better than dying in a military jihad. His sales pitch had been undermined. Shortly thereafter, he left me to join his father, who had just arrived at the mosque. Apparently his father seldom came to religious services, and my conversation partner was actively trying to guide him back to greater devotion. I never saw the young man again after that day, and I often wonder what became of him. I wonder if the hadith I taught him had changed the way he thought about his life as a Muslim and how to go about earning Allah's favor. That hadith was a rebuttal in the form of a story, or what we might call a counternarrative.

I do not know who taught that young Egyptian to think the way that he did or to believe so passionately that dying in jihad would bring him contentment and Allah's grace. He seemed to have so much ahead of him in life. He could do so much for the world around him. However, his ideas were hardly uncommon, as I knew of many writers, scholars, preachers, and even ordinary people who shared his views. Beyond the particular contextual form it took, his story was a familiar one, what I call the narrative of violence. Put briefly, it presents the idea that if you physically destroy the "Other"—the source of a community's discontent—then the country, the world, even God will produce the rewards—prosperity, prestige, and power—for the community.

The arguments of Islamist extremists, nationalist revolutionaries, and state governments may all have different historical contexts, concepts of authority, and circumstances, but the narrative solution they too often advocate is essentially one and the same: violence. It ultimately matters little who authorizes it or how it is justified. The important question is how human beings approach the problems in their societies. There are instances when a form of violence may prove necessary, such as preventing a crime, but as a means to redress sociopolitical grievances and create socioeconomic change the narrative of violence is a simplistic farce that perpetuates only further discontent. It is a form of false consciousness. The perpetuators of violence are actually enacting the source of their own discontent as an erroneous means to alleviate it.

Today people often talk about different kinds of wars and conflicts, such as a "war of ideas." The conservative pundit Bill O'Reilly, for example, often discusses something called a culture war, where liberals and conservatives struggle for influence and control over society. In *Searching for a King*, I write about "war" as an actual, intentional, and widespread armed conflict between political communities—entities that are either states or aspire to become states. Obviously war is a major theater for the enactment of violence (i.e., injurious physical force). However, I also address other forms of violence, such as violence against an authoritarian state by people seeking reform or change. Since I traverse back and forth between these cases, you might find a degree of conflation. To be clear, I am not focusing on interpersonal violence—the sort of deplorable violence that describes a man hitting his wife, for instance—but rather violence as a means to address sociopolitical grievances and bring about broad beneficial change, whether in war or as a mode of civil resistance. This latter sort of violence is often construed in terms of war, even if it is irregular and enacted by nonstate actors under unofficial authorities. This violence is not an isolated act but, akin to a war, a broad campaign to bring about specified goals, such as a new type of government or economic system.

Back in 1952 Cairo was the scene of a military coup against the Egyptian monarchy, led by a group called the Free Officers. The leader of the coup was an Arab nationalist, Gamal Abdel Nasser, whose portraits are still available for sale in Khan el-Khalili, Cairo's bustling grand bazaar. Nasser told his people that military might and the enactment of violence would expel the colonial occupiers and bring about Arab power, prestige, and prosperity. Likewise, the Islamist extremists who wanted to bring about a so-called Islamic state in Egypt during the tenure of Nasser's successor, Anwar Sadat, who was assassinated in 1981, believed that violence would transform Egypt into a new society that righteously earned Allah's favor. The religious rhetoric of the Islamist extremists may have differed from Nasser's revolutionary rhetoric in the 1950s, but the means and the underlying narrative were fundamentally the same. The results were the same as well: failure.

In *Searching for a King*, I adamantly reject the narrative of violence and present a counternarrative to it—namely, the narrative of nonviolence (described in chapter 3). This narrative should be familiar to anyone acquainted with the life and teachings of Martin Luther King Jr. or Mohandas Gandhi, albeit in very different contextual forms. Owing to the prominence of violent representations of Islam that have filled the contemporary mediascape, some readers may question or express skepticism about whether Islam is even compatible with such a narrative. Their skepticism, while understandable, is misguided.

I present my case for the compatibility of Islam with nonviolence by recounting the narratives and teachings of five modern Muslim champions of nonviolence from vastly different parts of the world. I suspect that most readers have never heard their stories before, and I explore why this may be the case. And finally I discuss the alternative possibilities that the adoption of nonviolence can offer to these societies, specifically in the form of interrelated complementary efforts such as microfinancing (chapter 9) and women's education programs (chapter 10).

Searching for a King concludes with a chapter titled "Jihad without Swords." Contrary to what one might expect, I do not reject the concept of jihad. In fact I affirm the importance of jihad, a term referring to a range of exerted efforts, as essential and inseparable from Islam. Indeed I argue that nonviolence is not only a legitimate form of jihad, as justified by the sacred texts, but its necessary form in the age of nuclear and chemical weapons, on the basis of a classical Islamic legal principle called *maslaha*, or the "public interest." Ultimately I hope this book will help to foster greater discussion among Muslims and non-Muslims about nonviolence and familiarize audiences with the great Muslim champions of nonviolence who rightfully belong alongside those more commonly known in the annals of history. Perhaps if these stories of Islamic nonviolence had been better known to us all, my conversation with that young man back in Egypt would have gone very differently.

1

Jihad and the Book

For many in the Western world, the tragic events and unforgettable images of 9/11 and the brutal wars in Iraq and Afghanistan have left the impression that Islam is somehow uniquely and irreconcilably violent. But as someone who on a daily basis studies Islam and its sacred texts, as well as religion as a whole, I find that impression troubling and misguided. It is vital to understand that all religions, including Islam, rest in the minds and hands of human beings. All religions are interpreted, and there are pivotal moments in history that dramatically shape those interpretations. People read and understand sacred texts (or any text for that matter) according to their own subjective and contextual needs and interests. Today the ancient Islamic concept of jihad, one of many products of interpretation, sits in flux. The Qur'an is being read by modern Muslims grappling with a very different world than the great scholars and jurists of the old empires.

There is an old saying attributed to the great seventh-century Muslim leader Ali ibn Abu Talib that points our discussion in the right direction. It came in response to a group of extremists, known as the Kharijites, after they opposed arbitration to bring an end to a tense battle in 657. The Kharijites argued that the Qur'an alone, Allah's revealed Word, should decide the outcome and not a human arbitrator. But Ali astutely responded, "The Qur'an is a book, covered, between two flaps, and it does not speak; it should therefore necessarily have an interpreter."[1] This is the core point: no sacred text, especially a very old one, has a single reading, no matter how literal or "by the book" a person claims to be. When we look at how Muslim proponents of nonviolence can and *have* approached the sacred texts of Islam, namely the Qur'an and the Hadith, we are talking about interpretation. The same is true when we talk about extremists such as al-Qaeda who carry out horrific acts of violence and invoke the very same texts. There is no absolute or "real" reading of a sacred text, and there will always be rival readings and evidence to support alternative readings. Thus it's useless to think about different approaches to the Qur'an as being correct or incorrect. Instead it's far more illuminating to think about different interpretations of religious ideas and texts in terms of persuasiveness and utility.

Beyond Islam

When it comes to nonviolence, virtually all religions face obstacles that have to be reconciled, including the religions of Martin Luther King Jr. and Mohandas K. Gandhi, arguably the two best-known modern champions of nonviolence. Violence is found in the sacred texts of nearly all religions; it simply depends on where one looks.

In parts of the Bible, for example, we find Yahweh depicted as a god who encourages warfare, even ordering his devotees to massacre defenseless men, women, and children in passages such as Numbers 31. Elsewhere, Yahweh kills countless children to persuade the tyrant Pharaoh to "let his people go." And after the Exodus, the Israelites slaughter the Canaanites and other inhabitants of the Promised Land with divine blessing. The Israelite king David, the messianic paradigm, is a great warrior who on one occasion killed two hundred Philistines and cut off their foreskins to present as a dowry (1 Samuel 18:27).

These instances are not limited to the Tanakh, or Old Testament, either. In the pages of the New Testament, Jesus of Nazareth, understood to be the incarnation of Yahweh and "Son of David" (Luke 18:38, Mark 10:47), is depicted in the Gospels as lashing the money changers, and his disciples carry swords. As related in the Book of Revelation, Jesus will descend at the end of time for a cataclysmic battle dressed in a robe covered in blood and wielding a sword to destroy the infidels.

Hindu sacred writings also contain considerable violent content. In the major Hindu epic, the Mahabharata, we find the Baghavad Gita, a hymn that tells the story of Arjuna and Lord Krishna. The Gita relates that Arjuna went out to war, and when he reached the battlefield he saw members of his family on the opposing side. Arjuna did not want to kill his kinsmen. But the god Krishna intervened, posing as his charioteer, and instructed Arjuna that he must fulfill his dharma and go out to fight on the battlefield. Elsewhere, the Hindu goddess Kali is depicted in texts and iconography with a belt of severed human limbs and a garland of severed human heads, devouring blood, and wielding fierce weapons in battle. At one time human sacrifices were even made to Kali by certain devotees known as *thuggees*, the origin of the term "thug."[2] This is only a very brief and selective glimpse at the sacred texts of Hinduism and Christianity, but I use these references to demonstrate that the inclusion of religious warfare in Islamic sacred texts is not at all unique. Islam's sacred texts are no more problematic than the aforementioned sacred texts of other religions, including those of King or Gandhi.

The historical-cultural landscape in which the sacred texts of all the world religions were written differs greatly from the international political order of the twenty-first century. The very nature of war—its purpose and its enactment—is radically different. This presents an important challenge for those who must interpret the sacred texts of Islam and grapple with its violent content.

The Qur'an and Hadith

The greatest interpretive challenge presented by Islam's sacred texts regarding violence is the content stemming from the Prophet Muhammad's war with the pagan Meccans and their allies during the Medinan period. This is the period that Muslim historians date from 622 to 632, during which some twenty-nine suras (chapters) of the Qur'an were revealed to Muhammad by Allah. All of the Qur'anic verses about warfare and fighting the infidels date from this period. Violent extremists obviously rely heavily on this content, even employing radical notions of abrogation (*naskh*) to nullify other Qur'anic verses about peace or that qualify war as purely defensive in nature.

Other material dating from the Medinan period is offered in the Hadith, the collected traditions about what the Prophet Muhammad is thought to have said and done (recorded and compiled in the ninth and tenth centuries). Hadith are particularly useful for proponents of violence because they exist as self-contained sayings and lack the same level of textual context offered by the Qur'an. They are also so great in number that they are often invoked and discarded at leisure.

One example of a hadith supporting violence is found in Sahih Bukhari, the most authoritative collection, dating from the ninth century. It relates that the Prophet Muhammad once said, "Know that Paradise is under the shade of swords." Another tradition, related in Sunan Abu Dawud, relates that the Prophet said, "He who does not join the war expedition, or equip, or looks well after a warrior's family when he is away, will be smitten by God with a sudden calamity." Even though these materials were not revealed by Allah like the Qur'an, they still carry transcendent status due to their alleged source (i.e., God's prophet), and that belief insulates the Hadith from certain kinds of criticism that has to be negotiated by people tasked with interpretation.

Historically Muslim scholars, faced with the challenge of interpreting Islam by reading and debating the sacred texts, have understood the concept of jihad as something that includes violent religious warfare or "holy war" sanctioned by Allah. The word itself actually means "struggle" or "exertion" (discussed further in chapter 11) and not "war." The word for "war" in Arabic, the language of the Qur'an, is actually *harb*. Other terms associated with war include *khasam* (quarrel), *wagha* (uproar), *qatl* or *qital* (kill or fight), and *sar'a* (wrestle). The Qur'an uses the word jihad, or its verb form *jahada*, to refer to exerted efforts or striving in the cause of God, including verses 9:73, 25:52, 29:68, and 66:9. But the word used for fighting in the Qur'an is actually qatl. We find qatl used in all of the Medinan verses about warfare, including 9:29, 9:123, 2:190–91, 2:216, 8:65–67, and the so-called "Verse of the Sword," 9:5. The Qur'an also uses the word harb in 47:4. Thus the notion that the word jihad narrowly refers to religious warfare is etymologically and textually incorrect. That said, the range of meaning that the word "struggle" or "striving" carries in the English language is similarly evident in the Arabic language, and jihad has been applied to a range of contexts, including violent military ones. The most obvious example of a military jihad is the initial wave of Muslim conquests during the seventh and eighth centuries that resulted in the creation of a vast empire spanning three continents.

After the establishment of a Muslim city-state in Medina in the final years of the Prophet's life, his political successors, the caliphs, expanded their realm outward from Islam's birthplace on the Arabian Peninsula into the lands of the two great superpowers of the seventh century, the Byzantine and Sasanian Empires. Critics of Islam frequently characterize this territorial expansion as an aggressive, bloodthirsty campaign to conquer and smite the infidels and capture booty, suggestive of the "true" nature of Islam. The problem is that the "victims" of the Muslim expansion were militant, conquering empires that waged wars for lands and booty and destroyed infidels—the same qualities that critics attribute to Islam. The Byzantines and Sasanians had actually waged a devastating war against each other for years prior to the Muslim expansion, leaving the two empires exhausted and ripe for defeat by the modest and unexpected Arab Muslim forces. In fact, when the Muslims conquered Egypt, the indigenous Egyptian Christians, adherents of the Coptic Church, welcomed the Muslims as liberators who would free them from the rule of the Byzantines, who regarded Coptic Christianity as a heresy. Likewise, when the Muslims crossed the Strait of Gibraltar (named after the Muslim conqueror Tariq ibn Ziyad—*Jabal al-Tariq* or "Mountain of Tariq"), the Jews of Spain welcomed the Muslims and fought alongside them as allies against the Visigoth Catholics who oppressed them as "Christ killers." These types of campaigns were the reality in the age of empires, political units that are fundamentally different from the nation-states that dominate the world we know today.

From Empires to Nation-States

Empires differed from nation-states in critical ways. They typically consisted of ruling hereditary dynasties, such as lines of kings or emperors. Due to their size and territories, they also governed multiethnic populations. These different peoples had different rights inside fluctuating and contested borders that relied on military force to preserve, enforce, and defend them from rival empires.[3] Imperial boundaries did not separate political units that possessed equal rights, but involved gradations of power and influence, and no neighbor was recognized as an equal.[4] While trade and taxation provided revenue sources, territorial conquest and war booty were major sources of income, especially for imperial soldiers. The inability of an empire to maintain a strong military force meant not only the loss of territory, but even the end of the empire itself. In cases where rulers mismanaged control of their armies (which was common) revolts occurred, and new dynasties or entirely new empires emerged with their own policies, legal systems, religions, and so on. Succession was often problematic, and control over military forces often dictated the outcomes of such disputes. In some cases, such as the vast empire of Timur (Tamerlane) in the fourteenth century, an empire might only last for a generation before fragmenting into rival warring kingdoms.

Despite the emergence of an Islamic empire in the late seventh century and the continued existence of such entities for the next thirteen hundred years, the Qur'an does not contain any notion of empire or any other system of governance. This means that the transition to the modern nation-state poses no inherent problem or conflict for Islam's sacred texts. If one can sift any system of governance from the pages of the Qur'an at all, it would be a tribal confederacy centered on a city-state—in other words, the simplistic Arab tribal system that emerged in the last decade of Muhammad's life in Medina. Nevertheless, the early adoption of an imperial system by Muhammad's successors, especially the Umayyad dynasty (661–750), which borrowed heavily from the Byzantine and Sasanian systems that preceded them in those lands, meant that the formative period of Islamic history occurred under the auspices of an empire. The core disciplines of Islamic thought, including jurisprudence (*fiqh*), and the compilation, codification, and analysis of oral traditions attributed to Muhammad (i.e., the Hadith), occurred in the context of imperial power. Therefore, the materials produced in the formative centuries of Islamic history, including so many of the seminal texts of Islamic scholarship, clearly reflect that reality, and they justify and facilitate the essential functions and tasks of the empire, including military conquest under the designation of jihad understood as "holy war."

The first great Islamic imperial dynasty was the Umayyads, ruling from Damascus, who employed formerly Byzantine Christian bureaucrats to help administer their imperial system (which was new to the tribal Arabs) that stretched from Spain to the Indus River Valley. During their reign, the Umayyad caliphs, who ruled as kings, replaced the tribal militias with regular army regiments, the most important of which were cavalry units. Those forces based in Syria, especially around Damascus, were the elite, best-equipped, and most favored soldiers, while distant provincial forces were less regarded and less reliable.[5] The primary means used by the Umayyads to ensure morale, loyalty, and control of these forces were religion and money. Nationalistic patriotism, with its notions of noble service and sacrifice for the country, did not yet exist. Interpretations of religion (i.e., Islam) that did not meet the needs of the empire were not patronized, relevant, or useful for that world. Readers will recall similar developments occurred in Christian thought, including notions of "just war," crusade, and inquisition, once Christianity became the religion of the Roman Empire (later the Byzantine Empire) and its successor kingdoms.

Imperial Islam continued under the Abbasid dynasty (750–1258), which overthrew the Umayyads in 750 and ruled from a new capital called Baghdad, in the land of Iraq. The Abbasid caliphs rose to power with the support of forces from the previously marginal and distant province of Khurasan. They were in power when the collections of hadith were compiled and codified in the ninth and tenth centuries, becoming the second most authoritative Islamic texts after the Qur'an, and when all four of the Sunni schools of law (*madhahib*) took shape. The imprint of the political reality of the age on these endeavors is indelible. Amid these struggles, rival Islamic empires also emerged, and by the tenth century no fewer than three Muslim caliphates existed at once, with capitals in Cordoba, Cairo, and Baghdad. These rival Muslim empires waged war on non-Muslim empires and on each other, invoking religion and competing for territory, power, and influence. This trend continued for the great empires to come, including the mighty military force of the Ottoman Turks.

The Ottomans, who later terrified Europe with their conquests, endured until the industrialized horrors of World War I and experienced the global transition into the nation-state system we know today. After World War II, most of the people of the world had become citizens of nation-states and served centralized governments within clearly delineated and recognized, fixed borders. In those borders, residents (or those legally resident) all had a nationality, such as "American," typically without any necessary ethno-religious identity. The transition to the nation-state system was often a violent and destructive one, though, because it required a radical reorganizing of realities on the ground. For example, the task of creating a nation-state for "the Turks" meant the removal or forceful assimilation of other populations with their own languages, religions, and cultures, such as the Armenians and Kurds. The nation-states of Greece and Turkey actually exchanged segments of their own populations by force in 1923—some 1.5 million people in all—to meet these ends.[6]

Subsequent developments in international law prohibited the military conquest and annexation of territory. Article 2 (4) of the United Nations Charter, ratified on October 24, 1945, prohibited the threat or use of force against the territorial integrity of another state and the acquisition of territory by force. It stipulates: "All members shall refrain in their international relations from the threat or use of force against the territorial integrity or political independence of any state, or in any other manner inconsistent with the purposes of the United Nations."[7] This was a radical change from the age of empires. The nation-state, as sovereign, enjoys a monopoly on violence within its fixed and internationally recognized borders but cannot violate the sovereignty of other states and may still face punitive action for certain actions within its own borders, such as human rights violations or ethnic cleansing. Despite fierce resistance, the growing internationalist order of the twenty-first century has increasingly propelled the concept of human rights to supersede those of citizens in a nation-state, sovereignty is negotiated or limited by intergovernmental organizations, and global markets and transnational corporations increasingly dictate the conditions of state economies. This is the emerging world to which this book is addressed.

Moving Forward

Muslim attitudes toward violence, revolving around the concept of jihad, have reached a pivotal and transformative historical moment. Muslims are living in an increasingly internationalist world of states very different from the old empires. Yet some have not relinquished old ways of thinking and have carried those worldviews into an industrialized world with horrific potential. If war and organized violence were an integral part of imperial life, where does it stand in the modern international age of nation-states? How has industrialization changed the nature of warfare and violence? These are important considerations. The formation of nation-states, as noted, was often a difficult and inorganic process, especially in Muslim lands where such political units were imposed by European colonial powers. This difficult political transformation left Muslims with no shortage of serious grievances that need resolution and strategies for change, such as the question of Palestine. Violence, as I will explore in the next chapter, remains one of the most common answers to these grievances, despite its devastating and counterproductive nature.

2

False Promise

To be clear, violence is not a uniquely Muslim problem—it is a worldwide *human* problem. The modern nation-state has altered our conceptions of how and when violence is appropriate, but it has definitely not diminished its popularity (despite improved international regulation). The social critic Hans Magnus Enzensberger once remarked that "animals fight, but they don't wage war; only man—unique among the primates—practices the large-scale, deliberate and enthusiastic destruction of his fellow creatures."[1] I don't think that anyone can deny that we, as a species, have an irresistible fascination with violence and war. We pay our hard-earned money to watch films about war, we play simulations and games about war, our children "play" war with toy guns, we build grand monuments to war, and we study the "great" wars in school. Even our gods wage war. This is not a recent development.

It seems that violence—acts of injurious physical force—has been a fixture of the human race since time immemorial. The Abrahamic sacred texts even relate that the firstborn son of the primordial father of humanity, Adam, was a murderer. Contemporary archeologists and anthropologists have found that throughout human history, interpersonal violence, especially among the males of the species, has been prevalent; cannibalism was widespread; and mass killings, murders, and assault injuries are all well documented.[2] Clearly, violence is a part of our everyday reality and history that we must all work to come to terms with.

There is evidence that violence and aggression are hard-wired into the human brain from the time it takes shape in the womb. Those innate physiological traits are shaped by a range of developmental factors, such as family life and economic class, over the course of a lifetime. They are also shaped by stories, or systems of stories, that we call narratives. Studies of narratives further suggest that humans understand their identities, societies, and worlds in terms of systems of stories (including nationalist and religious stories), that contain certain trajectories, forms, and archetypes.[3] We even use stories to process information about the nature of conflicts, grievances, and social ills. In what I call "the narrative of violence," human beings convey the idea that power, prestige, and prosperity can be achieved through the destruction of an Other—the source of existing discontent. In doing so, I make no significant distinction between the violence committed by nation-states, such as Iran, and the violence committed by nonstate actors, such as al-Qaeda, both of which use the same core narrative.

The narrative of violence can be broken down into some basic structural elements. A community is confronted by an Other that is the source of their discontent. The Other is so malicious and such a threat that it has to be physically and forcefully subdued. When the Other is subdued, the obstacle preventing the resolution of that discontent will disappear and contentment will be achieved. Adolf Hitler employed this narrative in its most extreme form as a solution to the perceived ills of German society, casting "non-Aryans" such as Jews and Roma as the Other. Today Islamist extremists, such as al-Qaeda, use the narrative of violence as the solution to the perceived ills of Muslim societies around the world.

Due to the fact that the nation-state, and nationalism along with it, was imposed by the colonial powers on the Muslim world less than a century ago (in some cases only decades ago), Muslim peoples often see themselves through prenationalist identities, namely those based on religion or tribe/ethnicity. Modern Christians, on the other hand, typically wage war and commit acts of violence in the name of nationalism and the flags that represent it, or what some scholars describe as "civil religion." In both cases, narratives are essential to the construction of social identities, forming the basis for how people distinguish themselves from an Other.

Violence saturates the stories we find in the media and cultures of many nations, including the United States. From the films we enjoy (e.g., *300*) to the games we play (e.g, *Medal of Honor*) and our national heroes (e.g., George Washington), there is an indisputable interest and attraction to war, particularly among young men. The lure of warfare is so strong that young men actually volunteer to engage in it, stirred by notions of nationalism, sacred duty, adventure, or social mobility. It's even been argued that human tendencies to engage in "coalitional aggression" is an advantageous trait fostered by natural selection, because young men use the resources available to them in order to attract a mate and reproduce. The argument further notes that in many cultures men can raise their status through participating in war, and in poor countries aggression may be the only resource young men have to gain a spouse. These observations suggest that governments should try to help young men find partners by improving access to resources for them to form families, as well as other strategies reducing the young male population in unstable countries, such as immigration programs.[4] These recommendations could prove useful, but sociopolitical grievances still need to be addressed. Problems require solutions, and the most common solution in societies around the world remains, at its core, the narrative of violence.

Violence

The history of the modern Muslim world, particularly after the colonial period when nation-states emerged on formerly imperial lands, affirms the words of Isaac Asimov, who once wrote, "Violence is the last refuge of the incompetent."[5] When we look at the core underlying narrative articulated by Islamist extremists, as well as the secular-nationalist revolutionaries of the twentieth century (most of whom had military backgrounds), it communicates the idea that power, prosperity, and prestige can be attained through violence. That narrative has proved to be a disastrous farce for those who attempt to enact it. From the Sudan to Afghanistan to the southern Philippines, the failure of violence to achieve success has been endemic, and it shows no signs of diminishing. Indeed, the narrative of violence and the actions that follow it have only further contributed to the debilitating underdevelopment, poverty, suffering, and humiliation that plague so many Muslims around the world and even foster controversial mass migration to the Western world.

When the Islamist extremist Osama bin Laden spoke to Muslims through his audio recordings and Internet videos, he disseminated this same narrative of violence. He told his Muslim audiences that the *umma* (community) can be powerful, prosperous, and blessed again if they only take up arms and destroy their enemies through violence or materially support the enactment of violence in their name. Islamist extremists do not speak of schools to educate future generations, of microfinancing programs to create jobs and small businesses, or of the quantitative data that shows the strong correlation between prosperous development and the social integration and education of women. Instead, Bin Laden and Islamist extremists have conveyed the crude simplicity of violence. In the process, contemporary extremist groups sound a lot like the secular-nationalist revolutionaries that preceded them, such as Gamal Abdel Nasser of Egypt, and who failed Muslim peoples in ways that are still being felt today.

After helping to rid Egypt of the British occupation following World War II (Britain was exhausted), Nasser, a career military man, rallied his people to the cause of Arab unity against imperialism and foreign exploitation. His primary target was the neighboring and nascent state of Israel, whose Jewish population was largely European in origin and whose existence in the former British Mandate of Palestine had been ratified by the United Nations in New York. For Nasser the state of Israel was a European colonial state occupying historically Arab land and property, as well as Muslim holy sites. As was true with his predecessor King Farouk in 1948, the solution that Nasser advocated was war, or more simply, violence. "We shall fight a regular war, a total war, a guerrilla war," Nasser declared in 1956. "Those who attack Egypt will soon realize they brought disaster upon themselves."[6]

In a period of less than twenty years, as Egypt struggled to keep pace with the modern world, Nasser led Egypt into wars against the state of Israel in 1956 and 1967, with hostilities persisting in between. Each time the Arab nations, including Egypt, entered into war with Israel, the Palestinians suffered, losing 78 percent of historical Palestine to Israeli control in 1948 and the other 22 percent in 1967.[7] The 1967 war, known as the Six-Day War, was particularly devastating to the Arab and Muslim world. The *naksa*, or "setback" as the Arabs called it, was not only a crushing defeat on the battlefield, but it also discredited the secular nationalists and bolstered the credibility of the Islamists. As the extremist ideologue of al-Qaeda Ayman al-Zawahiri later wrote, "The direct influence of the 1967 defeat was that a large number of people, especially youths, returned to their original identity: that of members of an Islamic civilization."[8] Yet in the years since the defeat, the Islamists have only continued to cling to the same simple narrative. And they continue to repeat the devastating mistake of enacting it. Reflecting on the impact that the 9/11 attacks on New York City and Washington had on the Palestinians, the prominent linguist and social critic Noam Chomsky observed in 2001:

> The atrocities of September 11 were a devastating blow for the Palestinians. . . . Israel is openly exulting in the "window of opportunity" it now has to crush Palestinians with impunity. In the first few days after the 9-11 attack, Israeli tanks entered Palestinian cities (Jenin, Ramallah, Jericho, for the first time), several dozen Palestinians were killed and Israel's iron grip on the population tightened.[9]

Meanwhile, the acts of violence committed by Palestinian extremists such as Hamas and the Palestinian Islamic Jihad have resulted in hard-handed reprisals, economic hardships, and disproportionate casualties for the Palestinians. What, we must ask, has this so-called jihad of the Islamists achieved for the Palestinian people? The answer is nothing but more checkpoints, border closings, barrier walls, bulldozing of homes, Israeli settlement expansions, assassinations, and Israeli military incursions.

Palestinian violence against Israel has given an ongoing excuse ("justification for hostilities") to prolong the Israeli occupation and gradual annexation of illegally occupied territory captured during the Six-Day War, including East Jerusalem. The faces of the Palestinian men and women on the "martyr" posters plastered around the slums of Gaza and the West Bank are not the heroes of an armed struggle, but the victims of it and the pervasive narrative of violence that supports it. The secular nationalists, such as the late Yassir Arafat, have proven to be no different than their Islamist counterparts in this respect. Arafat's campaign of violence did not succeed in statehood for the Palestinians. Even after his death, his campaign remains a failure. The world attention brought to the plight of the Palestinians by media coverage of terrorist attacks, such as the horrific murder of

Israeli athletes at the Munich games in 1972, has profoundly hurt the Palestinians far more than it ever benefited their nationalist cause.

With its prominent place in world politics, the failure of the narrative of violence is wide-reaching and far greater than the land of Palestine or the Middle East. The problem of the narrative of violence extends throughout the broader Muslim world, which is still struggling to emerge from the decline that followed the waning of the great Muslim empires of old. So whether we look at the societies of Nigeria, Sudan, Lebanon, Iran, Xinjiang, Pakistan, or elsewhere, we can find the same core narrative simmering on the corners of city streets and far away in rural farmlands. It promises that Muslims can win respect, dignity, justice, prosperity, and more through violence against a designated Other who is perceived as the source of their discontent. To investigate this phenomenon in global terms, it is important that we look at several places, including South Asia, where the majority of the world's Muslim population now lives, and nation-states such as Pakistan, a nexus for violent extremism that remains deeply involved with its war-torn neighbor, Afghanistan.

Lands of War

The U.S.-backed Afghan resistance to the Soviet occupation in the 1980s is often celebrated by Islamists as a triumphant (even miraculous) example of what Muslims can achieve when they take up arms to fight the infidel Other. The Soviet-Afghan War provides a perfect case study for the narrative of violence, as we can see it sprinkled throughout extremist treatises on the war. "The Russians withdrew, and power was left to the Afghan communist government, yet the mujahidin triumphed," al-Zawahiri wrote. "If the fighting stops, the disbelievers dominate, and the *fitna* [discord] which is *shirk* [idolatry], spreads," warned Abdullah Azzam, the ideologue of the Afghan jihad, in his own piece.[10] "We have already seen lofty examples of new blossoms," Azzam further states in praise of the benefits of the war, "which Allah has steered until they ripened in the kiln of the battlefield, and became matured by its heat."[11]

What triumphs or "blossoms" are the Islamists referring to exactly? There are few places on our planet that can match the misery and destruction brought about by violence than the scarred land of Afghanistan. During the Soviet-Afghan War an estimated one million Afghans were killed, over five million fled abroad, over two million were internally displaced, and the country's infrastructure was left in ruins.[12] After the Soviet forces withdrew in 1989, Afghanistan was left to the Islamists to rebuild and create prosperity for the diverse Muslim peoples that reside there. But the Islamists demonstrated their incompetence and brought about only further death, destruction, and chaos. Their forces, so-called mujahideen ("holy warriors"), splintered into rival warlord factions along ethnic and political lines, overthrew the pro-Soviet regime in Kabul, submitted the country to the infamous barbaric period of Taliban rule, and plunged it into the civil war that has continued to the present.[13]

Today Afghanistan is home to over one million people with disabilities, including 250,000 maimed by land mines or the delayed detonation of "unexploded ordnance."[14] "The widespread and indiscriminate use of mines during more than two decades of conflict has left Afghanistan as one of the most heavily contaminated countries in the world," according to a 2009 report. Despite active demining programs run by the United Nations and other agencies (mainly since 2002), 4,924 hazardous areas totaling an estimated 720 square kilometers still remained by the summer of 2008. Approximately 50 percent of land mine victims in Afghanistan have been children. Land mines have also had a profound economic impact on the already impoverished country, because the mines prevent land from being used for agriculture, trade, housing construction, and the grazing of livestock.[15]

Living conditions in Afghanistan are appalling. According to the Office of the UN Human Rights Commissioner, Afghanistan has the second-highest maternal mortality rate in the world, the third-highest rate of child mortality, only 23 percent of Afghans have access to safe drinking water, and only 24 percent above the age of fifteen can read and write.[16] One could go on citing the grim statistics about unemployment and poverty levels, but it is already abundantly clear that the situation in Afghanistan is dire and deplorable. When we observe these conditions, and the well-documented horrors of the Taliban regime, it is impossible not to ask what the narrative of violence, as espoused by the various Islamist factions, has done for the people of Afghanistan. It appears to have done nothing beneficial. The people of Afghanistan are among the most impoverished and uneducated in the world.

Meanwhile in Egypt, home to the largest population in the Middle East, local Islamist extremist groups such as the Gama'a al-Islamiyya, or al-Jihad (merged with al-Qaeda), have long argued that the prosperity of Egypt would only come about when the "infidel" regime (since toppled by the Arab Spring) is destroyed and replaced with an "Islamic" government through violence (under the banner of jihad). Numerous terrorist attacks and the allocation of Egypt's limited resources to protecting civil society (including its lucrative tourism industry) were the immediate result. According to a 2005 nationwide estimate, 20 percent of Egypt's population lived below the poverty line, and a generous 2009 estimate puts Egypt's unemployment rate at just under 10 percent.[17] In rural southern Egypt, poverty is as high as 41 percent.[18] Some attention has been given to this sort of data as a means to criticize Egypt or as a way to understand the impact of certain social conditions on radicalization, especially among youths. The point I want to emphasize, however, is the fact that this narrative has offered no solutions to alleviate these conditions beyond lofty religious propaganda, and that same narrative threatens to make these conditions exponentially worse. Nevertheless, the narrative has shown remarkable resiliency by deferring blame for ongoing social ills and suffering to the malevolent Other.

In South Asia, Pakistan has recently been described by international analyst Fareed Zakaria as the world center of Islamist terrorism.[19] Home to an enormous number of extremist groups, including at one time Osama bin Laden himself, and a historical center of Islamist thought (e.g., Islamist ideologue Abul Ala Mawdudi), Pakistan is perilously close to becoming a failed state. Most alarming of all, Pakistan possesses nuclear warheads. The "father" of Pakistan's nuclear weapons program, A. Q. Khan, is popularly regarded as a national hero. Established as a nation-state in 1947, the country has an estimated 175 million people, 24 percent of whom live below the poverty line, and over 15 percent are unemployed.[20] High risk of infectious diseases and high rates of infant mortality also plague the population. The nationwide literacy rate is estimated at only 49.9 percent; among women, the number drops to 36 percent.[21] The Pakistani government, meanwhile, spends more on military expenditures than education and continuously demonstrates its incompetence by allowing, or even encouraging, the narrative of violence to thrive among its people. Pulitzer Prize–winning columnist Nicholas Kristof noted in the *New York Times*:

People with links to Pakistan have been behind a hugely disproportionate share of international terror incidents over the last two decades: [including] the 1993 and 2001 World Trade Center attacks; Richard Reid's failed shoe bombing in 2001; the so-called Bojinka plot in 1995 to blow up 12 planes simultaneously; the 2005 London train and bus bombings; the 2001 attacks on the Indian Parliament; and attacks on two luxury hotels and a Jewish center in Mumbai in 2008 [and most recently the failed Times Square bombing by Faisal Shahzad in 2010].[22]

There seems to be little or no sense among many of these communities of how people can improve the daily conditions of their lives or challenge injustices or resolve sociopolitical grievances, outside of enacting violence. I see it as a failure to understand that the narrative of violence is a mechanism of false consciousness that obscures and conceals the real sources of their poverty, humiliation, and underdevelopment in the modern world. The only people who benefit from violence are those small numbers of individuals who profit from the sale of weaponry or who acquire power, land, or resources through its enactment. Violence does not benefit society or the community as a whole.

In Somalia, the most turbulent country in East Africa, violence is the everyday social reality. Competing factions struggle to overcome each other with greater levels of violence, while international aid organizations are unable to work effectively in such a dangerous and unstable environment. As the Islamists blame the "infidels" and "apostates," they fail to recognize their own suicidal false consciousness. Their commitment to violence is the principal source of Somalia's ongoing suffering and chaos. As noted in a 2007 report, the violent conditions in Somalia are so bad that "people fleeing the capital have been reduced to renting trees for shelter."[23] As we would expect, the social conditions that the people of Somalia have to emerge from are terribly disturbing. The nationwide literacy rate in Somalia is less than 38 percent, which may be a generous estimate.[24] Life expectancy for Somalis is less than fifty years of age (which is still better than Afghanistan), and the country has the sixth-highest infant mortality rate in the world. Poverty and unemployment data is difficult to determine, but Somalia is widely believed to be one of the most impoverished regions in the world.

Religion and Violence

While violence is a universal trait of our species, the role of religion, especially important in regions where the nation-state remains weak, makes it all the more alarming and more challenging to dissipate. Religion, in this case Islam, encodes human preferences, customs, and worldviews with transcendent or divine status. By attributing the narrative to a divinely revealed text (i.e., the Qur'an), the narrative of violence is insulated from criticism and assumes an aura of truth and authority that transcends mere human opinion. As the noted historian of religion Bruce Lincoln has stated, "Religious discourse can recode virtually any content as sacred, ranging from the high-minded and progressive to the murderous, oppressive, and banal, for it is not any specific orientation that distinguishes religion, but rather its metadiscursive capacity to frame the way any content will be received and regarded."[25] This means that religion can take almost anything—from the clothes you wear all the way to your views on government—and justify it as part of the proper cosmic order of things. As such, despite the data reviewed, the narrative of violence can successfully resist criticism when framed by religion in ways that other narratives or arguments may not.

One method of refuting the narrative is subverting transcendent claims by attacking all of religion, as Richard Dawkins or the late Christopher Hitchens have done, but doing so may only bolster the claims of Islamist extremists who contend that the enemy Other is fighting the entire religion (not simply the extremists). Classical theories that depict a historical trend toward secularization have also proved to be incorrect, and, as some scholars have argued, societies simply must find ways to cope with the reality of "public religions."[26] Another insightful study, by political scientist Leonard Binder, has argued that political liberalism in the modern Muslim world will ultimately depend on the success of a vigorous Islamic liberalism.[27] If we situate these arguments in terms of narrative studies, countering the narrative of violence articulated by extremists might be possible if we encourage effective counternarratives that refute its claims, while simultaneously providing an alternative that rigorously meets the religious "litmus test" among Muslim audiences.

The narrative of violence has countless manifestations in different historical and cultural contexts. Among contemporary Islamist extremists, the narrative of violence has assumed the form of the jihad against the "enemies of Islam." For example, the twentieth-century Egyptian Islamist ideologue Sayyid Qutb wrote that "since the objective of the message of Islam is a decisive declaration of man's freedom, not merely on the philosophical plane but also in the actual conditions of life, it must employ jihad."[28] In this particular manifestation, the narrative is built on the content of the Qur'an and *sunna* (exemplary custom) of the Prophet Muhammad (as derived from the Hadith and sacred biographies), and it expands from there by incorporating a wide range of interpretive and political considerations, such as who the enemy might be. Political expediency always figures prominently in the narrative. It will also incorporate notions of martyrdom that help to displace reservations among people who are afraid of dying or making the sacrifices involved. Functionalist approaches to religion have correctly perceived the capacity of religions to provide solace for human suffering (e.g., you'll be rewarded in heaven) and to stabilize social norms by attributing their origins to a transcendent source (e.g., gay marriage is illegal because God said so in the Bible). Both of these elements are readily employed in the Islamist narrative of violence. Fighting the Other is part of God's plan, the Islamists contend, and participants will go to heaven and receive the greatest rewards for participating and dying in the jihad against the malevolent Other.

Are the Qur'an and the Hadith uniquely and irreconcilably violent? The sacred texts of Islam certainly offer ample material for Islamist extremists to selectively use in their particular invocations or manifestations of the narrative of violence. The three Abrahamic religions all contain stories of God's righteous servants slaughtering unbelievers and sinners. In addition, many of the prophets featured in the sacred texts, who are cited as figures to be emulated, were warriors who fought on the battlefield and killed for their god. Thus it should not surprise us to find adherents of the Abrahamic religions, including Muslims, utilizing religious stories to promote and advocate violence.

Muhammad began his prophetic mission at the age of forty in the city of Mecca. For twelve years, he preached his Abrahamic message to anyone who would listen among the tribal peoples of Arabia but achieved only modest results. His teachings were enough to disturb the status quo, though, and persecution of his small group of monotheistic followers ensued. In 622 Muhammad and his followers fled Mecca and resettled in the agricultural city of Yathrib (later known as Medina). In his new home, Muhammad had far more success, and he rose to be the leader of the city. As a statesman, the Prophet was responsible for military matters, and war with the hostile pagans of Mecca soon followed. All of the verses in the Qur'an regarding war and fighting the unbelievers date from this period. The most infamous passage on warfare from the Qur'an is the so-called "Verse of the Sword" (9:5): "But when the forbidden months are past, then fight and slay the pagans wherever you find them, and seize them, harass them, and lie in wait for them in every stratagem of war; but if they repent, and establish the prayers and give the alms, then open the way for them: for God is Forgiving, Merciful." Although there is an obvious historical context for this passage, it is not difficult for content like this to be applied to contemporary circumstances through simple analogies.

An Example of the Narrative

No Muslim was more infamous in the Western world for his advocacy of violence than the late Osama bin Laden. Indeed, there was great jubilation in the United States with the news of his death at the hands of U.S. Navy SEALs. The record of his many media statements provide abundant examples of the narrative of violence framed in terms of fighting the "infidel enemies of Islam." The following passages are excerpts from one audio statement made by him in March of 2009 regarding the ongoing conflict in war-torn Somalia. In the statement, he clearly identifies an Other as the source of Muslim discontent and suffering, and advocates violence against the Other as the sole means to resolve that discontent. The passage concludes with a citation from the Qur'an designed to legitimize his message with transcendent authority and status:

> All intelligent people are aware of American combating of Islam, and its past rejection of its establishment in Somalia, as well as in Iraq and Afghanistan . . . I address my brothers the Mujahideen, the honest sons of Somalia, and call on them to continue their steps on the path of jihad. Global Infidelity is facing predicaments and crises the likes of which it has not seen for many decades, so persevere and be resolute, for you are one of

the important armies in the Mujahid Islamic battalion, and are the first line of defense for the Islamic world in its southwestern part; and your patience and resolve supports your brothers in Palestine, Iraq, Afghanistan, the Islamic Maghreb, Pakistan and the rest of the fields of jihad; and their patience and resolve in the face of the same enemy—America and its allies.[29]

Here bin Laden expressed his narrative of violence in global terms. Even though the primary audience was in the land of Somalia, with its particular circumstances, Bin Laden explicitly linked his narrative solution to numerous fronts around the world, including Palestine, Afghanistan, and Pakistan. They are all "the fields of jihad." Absent are the important historical, cultural, political, legal, and economic factors at play in each unique regional case. Violence is the solution all around.

There are, of course, different gradations of violence. Punching someone is not the same as detonating a bomb in a crowded marketplace. The violence advocated by Osama bin Laden was obviously the more extreme form. He was not interested in fistfights. Bin Laden's narrative of violence proposed that the Other must be physically destroyed. It did not necessarily equate with genocide, but it did constitute the intent to commit lethal violence. For example, the assassination attempt against Nobel laureate Naguib Mahfouz in Cairo in 1994 was not any less violent because Mahfouz survived the stabbing he received in the neck. The violence was intended to destroy him as a representative of the malevolent Other. Bin Laden's statements called on Muslims to fight and kill Americans and their "Zionist-Crusader" allies. This violence also had symbolic considerations. The Twin Towers were not targeted purely for the sake of mass casualties, but for the profound psychological and economic impact their destruction would have on the United States and the world. The attack literally altered the most famous skyline in the country, and it is difficult not to be reminded of it whenever one looks at a view of New York City. The day-to-day "fields of jihad," however, often lack the symbolic considerations that the grand plotters of attacks like September 11 undertake.

The language of violence employed by Islamist extremists is often disturbingly graphic. Shaykh Abdullah El-Faisal (born Trevor William Forest) is an Islamist extremist who was arrested in Britain and deported for his violent exhortations. During audio recordings of el-Faisal's trial, he is heard telling Muslim audiences to kill Hindus, Jews, and other non-Muslims like "cockroaches."[30] El-Faisal was also recorded saying, "You are only allowed to use nuclear weapons in that country which is 100 percent unbelievers."[31] In another example, the Jordanian Islamist extremist Abu Musab al-Zarqawi decapitated an American civilian contractor in Iraq named Nicholas Berg on video and declared, "So we tell you that the dignity of the Muslim men and women in Abu Ghraib and others is not redeemed except by blood and souls; you will not receive anything from us but coffins after coffins . . . slaughtered in this way."[32] In yet another instance, Trevor "Omar" Brooks, a British extremist also known by the name Abu Izzadeen, stood before an audience at a public debate in the United Kingdom in 2007 and declared, "We are the Muslims. We drink the blood of the enemy, and we can face them anywhere. That is Islam and that is jihad."[33]

This sort of language of violence dehumanizes the Other as an inferior, animal-like being. El-Faisal referred to killing the Other like cockroaches and endorsed the use of nuclear weapons against them as a faceless whole. Al-Zarqawi spoke of slaughtering the Other in a way that one might treat livestock at a slaughterhouse. Brooks spoke of drinking the blood of the Other, as if it were a grisly commodity to be consumed (despite the fact that it is forbidden to consume blood according to Islamic dietary law). The level of abstraction evident in these statements suggests a serious psychological disconnect with reality. Sociopaths use this sort of language. As one study of antisocial personality disorder (sociopathy) has noted, "terrorism is the ideal occupation for a person who is possessed of blood lust and no conscience, because if you do it just right, you may be able to make a whole nation jump."[34]

Osama bin Laden typically exhibited greater reserve in the language he used, at least more so than the preceding individuals cited, but the narrative of violence conveyed in his messages carries the same sociopathic abstractions of the Other. The American is the "Crusader" who invades and subjugates his targets as part of a single-minded malevolent horde. He (or she) is the Other at war with Islam. Bin Laden warned Muslims: "You are threatened in everything you possess—in your persons and wealth—and are even threatened in the greatest thing you have: your religion."[35] His solution to this perceived worldwide threat to the Muslim world was straightforward: "Let each of us protect his garrison, and heal his chest by killing the trespassers."[36] The Crusaders can only be met with violence, and, he claimed, dutiful violence would bring glory and triumph to the modern Muslim world.

Implications

If violence is such a destructive farce, why do human beings still insist on engaging in it? The famous political theorist Hannah Arendt presented us with an interesting answer. She argued that "the chief reason warfare is still with us is neither a secret death wish of the human species, nor an irrepressible instinct of aggression, nor, finally and more plausibly, the serious economic and social dangers inherent in disarmament, but the simple fact that no substitute for this final arbiter in international affairs has yet appeared on the political scene."[37]

Arendt's observation is astute; however, it seems to me rather dated, and I would contest the characterization of violence as the "final arbiter" of affairs. For all their faults, globalization and the emerging internationalist order have meant that the world is far more intertwined and interdependent than ever before. The possibilities for punitive and preventative action are therefore broader than at any other time in human history. The possibilities are numerous, but the alternatives to warfare and violence are complex. Violence, on the other hand, carries emotional power and remains a readily understood act that provides immediate and tangible results in the form of corpses and physical destruction. Most cultures in the world, including that of the United States, assign tremendous glory and prestige to participating in military campaigns. Brightly colored ribbons and highly polished medals are even given to those who are wounded or who lead successful attacks against the enemy. Military heroism can even carry an individual to the highest political offices. And for certain members of the status quo, tremendous economic incentives are involved, in the form of lucrative military contracts. President Dwight D. Eisenhower famously described the business of war as the "military-industrial complex" and rightly warned the American people of its interests.

Muslims involved in campaigns of violence are seldom the manufacturers of the instruments of violence (i.e., weapons) used in conflicts. Someone else is typically profiting from the AK-47s, explosives, or rocket launchers used by violent extremists. But we should not overstate the business of war in this case, especially when we talk about the unconventional warfare most nonstate actors or Islamist extremists carry out. One of the most potent weapons currently used in the extremist arsenal is the improvised explosive device (IED). It can be made with common, everyday products with devastating results. The IED is not the product of a military industry. Instead, in seeking a solution to Muslim discontent, we need to look at the narrative of violence that informs the course of action that results in the construction and deployment of such a weapon as an IED to kill, maim, destroy, or terrorize.

One of the reasons that the narrative of violence has remained so persistent in the modern Muslim world, despite its obvious failings, is a general lack of awareness regarding alternative strategies and methods for the resolution of grievances. With this in mind, I would modify Arendt's observation to argue instead that alternative substitutes remain outside of general popular awareness and that nonviolence has been erroneously dismissed as weak or ineffective out of common ignorance or by those who have political and economic interests for the ongoing perpetuation of violence. We should remember too that despite the emergence of Martin Luther King Jr. in the United States and Mohandas Gandhi in India, these societies are still plagued by a considerable degree of violence, even from religious extremists. Both men were assassinated by their own countrymen. The problem of violence, if it is not already clear, most certainly goes beyond the Muslim world.

To probe these issues further, I'll explore the concept of nonviolence and whether it is useful as an alternative means for addressing a range of sociopolitical grievances and conflicts, including its limits in the face of genocide. By nonviolence, I am referring specifically to nonviolent resistance and various forms of civil disobedience and social protest. I am not at all referring to passive nonresistance. And returning to the question of religion, I will also look at Islamic frameworks for nonviolence, especially in terms of the sacred texts, by looking closely at several little-known historical cases of modern Muslim scholars, leaders, and activists who have championed nonviolence. Many of these figures, if not all of them, will probably be new to Western readers.

3

Nonviolence

Nonviolence is a radical and controversial concept that is frequently misunderstood. When viewed correctly, it's as dangerous to the powers that be as any state army or terrorist threat. Nonviolence is not infallible or an invincible alternative to violence, however—far from it. There are definitely limits to its utility. Successful nonviolence requires great strength of character, perseverance, and discipline, which is more than the minimum required to commit an act of violence (thus lessening its popular appeal). At its core, nonviolence is a means of awakening a sense of injustice and moral shame in the supporters of a power structure, showing them that they have more to gain by ending injustice and oppression than by maintaining them.[1] Therefore, nonviolence cannot be successful in secret; it has to exist under the watchful eye of the world. It is a form of communication. In the twenty-first century, the emergence of new media such as online video has provided contemporary practitioners of nonviolence with arguably the greatest tools for success in history. A renewed investigation of nonviolence is thus certainly overdue.

If we think about nonviolence in terms of a narrative, it has a distinct structural form that is very different from our other narrative. A community is confronted by a dominant power structure or social faction that enforces the conditions of that community's discontent. Those in power seek to maintain their dominance over the community. When the means used to maintain the power structure's dominance are exposed as unjustified through nonviolent confrontation, the subsequent loss of prestige causes the power structure to falter and the conditions of the community are reformed justly, according to the popular will and means of the community.

Exposing the unjust means of the power structure requires the isolation of its actions, eliminating any opportunity for the authorities to rhetorically invoke a justification for their hostilities on the basis of reciprocity. Doing so may require members of the community to endure harassment, incarceration, abuse, injury, or even death at the hands of those in power. The coercive acts of violence against members of the community must thereafter be witnessed and transmitted as images or stories in order to damage or eliminate the prestige of the oppressors. If successful, the damage to their prestige will result in damage to their wealth, influence, and status through a range of ramifications such as international economic boycotts. This will demonstrate the interdependence of global societies and the inability of the power structure to maintain its standing for any prolonged period in isolation.

Today nonviolent resistance enjoys the widest array of means in history. These means can be categorized broadly into two camps: direct action and indirect action. In this chapter, I not only explore the concept of nonviolence, its modern history, limitations, and utility, but direct and indirect forms of action in the context of the aforementioned narrative. In the process, I will explore a range of cases on a practical and strategic level that can help explain the concept further. Religious frameworks for nonviolence are commonplace; however, a detailed study of nonviolence in the Islamic context will serve as the subject of later chapters.

A Brief Modern History

The concept of nonviolence has existed for centuries, dating to (at least) the time of the Indian sages Vardhamana (or Mahavira; d. ca. 527 BCE), the founder of Jainism, and Siddhartha Gautama (d. ca. 483 BCE), the founder of Buddhism, assuming that these figures are actual historical personalities. The modern history of nonviolence, however, begins with the sweeping social transformation brought about by the Industrial Revolution. Industrialization resulted in rapid urbanization and the transformation of labor and daily living conditions, especially among the lower classes. The impact of industrialization on human history was nothing short of profound, and it was felt in virtually every corner of society. One such area was in the media and publishing industry, which utilized the rapid production capabilities of the factory and the broad distribution channels provided by networks of roads and railways, and, eventually, radio broadcasts. Another area profoundly transformed by industrialization was warfare. The capabilities of industrialized warfare were fully realized in the horrors of World War I, in which over 15 million people perished. The world had never seen anything comparable.

Elihu Burritt, a nineteenth-century American blacksmith and self-taught linguist, began a series of publications in the 1840s that promoted the peaceful resolution of conflicts, as well as a Christian conception of nonviolence with millennial overtones. His small newspaper, *The Christian Citizen*, was reportedly "the first newspaper in America that devoted any considerable portion of its space to the advocacy of the cause of peace."[2] A skilled communicator, Burritt also launched the League of Universal Brotherhood (LUB), a Christian organization that reached nearly thirty thousand members (including women) and four hundred branches by the summer of 1848.[3] Each member of the LUB had to make a peace pledge: "I do hereby pledge myself never to enlist or enter into any army or navy, or to yield any voluntary support or sanction to any war, by whomsoever or for whatsoever proposed, declared, or waged."[4] Strengthened by the organization's support, Burritt convened numerous meetings in growing European and American cities to discuss issues including disarmament, abolition, the creation of a congress of nations, and international correspondence between citizens, which he called "people diplomacy."[5] But his attempts to prevent the outbreak of wars all failed. Disheartened by the American Civil War, he left America and served President Abraham Lincoln as U.S. consular agent for the city of Birmingham, England. When he returned five years later, he lived out the rest of his life as a farmer and writer. But despite Burritt's relative failures, his ideas and writings managed to reach one of the most important modern champions of nonviolence, Leo Tolstoy.[6]

Tolstoy is best known as the author of *War and Peace* and other classic literary works, but his commitment to nonviolence remains one of the most enduring features of his eccentric life. In his treatise *The Kingdom of God Is within You*, Tolstoy argued that "war, that is, the wounding and killing of men, is inconsistent with a religion founded on peace and good will toward men."[7] After joining the army as a young man and serving in Russia's campaigns in the Caucasus and the Crimean War (1853–1856), Tolstoy concluded that his energies were far more useful in the field of education. Devotion to family life and writing followed. Though no longer a soldier, war remained a fixture of his literary works. Contrary to the dominant historical narratives of his time, however, Tolstoy treated war (and history as a whole) as an assortment of small contingencies and choices made by ordinary people that form a chaotic confluence of events. In doing so, Tolstoy revealed his preference for particularities over abstractions and rejected the idea of grand systems of rules that claim to govern the infinite complexities of life.[8] In light of these views, Tolstoy was deeply troubled by the underlying meaning of life and death, and chose to devote himself to the teachings of Jesus Christ.

However, Tolstoy rejected the official institutional churches as corrupt deviations of the "true message" of Jesus. In fact, his views on the errors of normative Christianity led to his excommunication by the Russian Orthodox Church in 1901.[9] Tolstoy rejected virtually all of the doctrines and rituals that form the basic features of the Christian religion, including the sacraments, belief in miracles, the theology of the Incarnation and the Trinity, as well as much of the Old Testament and New Testament.[10] Tolstoy, rather, found meaning in a selective, human image of Jesus, especially the ascetic message of the Sermon on the Mount.[11] Accordingly, Tolstoy advocated an uncompromising commitment to peace and condemned government systems for their dependence on violence and coercion. "The 'right' upon which the wealthy have their ownership of land, their appropriation of the fruits of other men's toil, and their exactions of taxes, have nothing in common with justice," he wrote. "All three are based only on violence maintained by military force."[12]

Tolstoy's contemplation of violence led him to a deep belief in "nonresistance to evil." The core of Tolstoy's beliefs can be summarized as: love your enemy, swear no oaths, do not lust, bear no malice, and do not resist evil, which inevitably leads to the abolition of all compulsory legislation, police, prisons, armies, and, ultimately, to the abolition of the state itself.[13] Violence or physical coercion is entirely illegitimate. As Tolstoy wrote in a letter to Ernest Howard Crosby: "People know it is wrong to use violence, but they are so anxious to continue to live a life secured by 'the strong arm of the law,' that, instead of devoting their intellects to the elucidation of the evils which have flowed, and are still flowing, from admitting that man has a right to use violence to his fellow-men, they prefer to exert their mental powers in defense of that error."[14] Tolstoy's beliefs, which included vegetarianism, gained a small following of individuals who came to be known as the Tolstoyans, often described as pacificist anarchists. Tolstoy's advice and guidance was constantly sought by people outside his small circle of devotees, mainly through letters.

In 1908 Tolstoy wrote a letter to an Indian anti-imperialist activist, Tarak Nath Das, in order to encourage the use of nonviolence against British colonial rule. "If the people of India are enslaved by violence it is only because they themselves live and have lived by violence," he wrote, "and do not recognize the eternal law of love inherent in humanity." The letter subsequently appeared in the Indian newspaper *Free Hindustan* and attracted the attention of a young Indian lawyer in South Africa, Mohandas K. Gandhi.

Gandhi entered into correspondence with Tolstoy only briefly before Tolstoy's death but studied his writings with great enthusiasm, especially *The Kingdom of God Is within You*. He referred to Tolstoy as "one of the clearest thinkers in the western world, one of the greatest writers, one who as a soldier has known what violence is and what it can do. . . . His logic is unassailable."[15] In South Africa Gandhi named the ashram he established in Durban the "Tolstoy Farm."[16] Despite his profound admiration, however, Gandhi differed with Tolstoy on several points. Most notably, Gandhi advocated nonviolent resistance to induce social change in the state.

Gandhi was a nationalist and did not share Tolstoy's anarchist views. Rather, Gandhi sought to reform the conditions of society, especially unjust and discriminatory laws, through a militant form of nonviolent resistance described as *satyagraha* ("truth force"), employing direct action that included strikes, marches, boycotts, and acts of civil disobedience.[17] In India he initiated a mass campaign of nonviolence against the British occupation of his country and advocated Hindu-Muslim unity and caste integration in support of the nationalist cause. "Nonviolence is the greatest and most active force in the world," Gandhi wrote. "One person who can express nonviolence in life exercises a force superior to all the forces of brutality."[18] As an active practitioner of nonviolence, Gandhi possessed the courage and discipline necessary for its enactment, but the masses that responded to his leadership did not always share his abilities.

During an early campaign against the Rowlatt Act in 1919, which prolonged Britain's emergency wartime measures in India indefinitely, numerous demonstrations around the country degenerated into mob violence and bloodshed, particularly in the Punjab.[19] The bloodiest incident took place at the sacred city of Amritsar, where British-Indian soldiers under Brig. Gen. Reginald Dyer massacred hundreds of scattering men, women, and children who had gathered in protest. Violent reprisals for what became known as the Jallianwala Bagh massacre ensued in the following days.

Gandhi's principle of satyagraha had to be taught, and the culture of violence, fueled by raw human emotion, had to be remedied through conscious self-awareness and discipline. Participants had to be extraordinarily brave and willing to die for the cause without resorting to retaliatory violence. Individuals had to possess a willingness to accept unjust imprisonment, abuse, and brutality. The power of this policy of self-sacrifice was evident in the fallout from the Jallianwala Bagh massacre. News of it alienated millions of previously loyal supporters and admirers of the British, and even Indian Anglophiles became converts to Gandhi's revolutionary leadership and methods.[20] By March 1930 Gandhi's famous anti-salt tax march to the ocean reflected the growing strength of his movement and the increasing implementation of its strict principles. Millions of Indians walked to the ocean, where they made lumps of sea salt to use instead of British tax-inflated salt.[21] Some sixty thousand arrests, including Gandhi's, followed for violating the salt monopoly and overwhelmed the colonial prisons. In the years thereafter, Gandhi produced numerous writings and delivered many speeches in response to critics and sincere questioners alike, providing his insights into nonviolence as he continued his satyagraha campaigns against the British even as India entered into World War II.

In 1950 Martin Luther King Jr. was introduced to the teachings of Gandhi during a sermon by Mordecai Johnson, president of Howard University, who had returned from a trip to India. "His message was so profound and electrifying," King wrote, "that I left the meeting and bought a half-dozen books on Gandhi's life and works."[22] King had been highly skeptical of the ethical pacifism articulated in parts of the Gospels as a means to transform society. He wrote, "The 'turn the other cheek' philosophy and the 'love your enemies' philosophy were only valid, I felt, when individuals were in conflict with other individuals; when racial groups and nations were in conflict, a more realistic approach seemed necessary."[23] But Gandhi's concept of satyagraha profoundly changed King's perspective, and he saw how "utterly mistaken" he had been. He would later write:

> I was particularly moved by his Salt March to the sea and his numerous fasts. The whole concept of *satyagraha* was profoundly significant to me. . . . Love for Gandhi was a potent instrument for social and collective transformation. It was in this Gandhian emphasis on love and nonviolence that I discovered the method for social reform that I had been seeking.[24]

King thus adopted the militant nonviolent resistance of Gandhi, which recognized the legitimacy of the state and the law. Tolstoy's anarchist Christian pacifism, a target of a forceful critique of nonviolence by Christian theologian Reinhold Niebuhr, did not appeal to King or meets his needs. His study of Gandhi led him to conclude that "true pacifism is not nonresistance to evil, but nonviolent resistance to evil," because Gandhi "resisted evil with as much vigor and power as the violent resister."[25] The application of Gandhi's concept of satyagraha to the endemic racial violence, discrimination, and segregation in the United States, particularly in the Jim Crow South, proved to be revolutionary.

In 1955 King began his implementation of nonviolent resistance against the southern white power structure in Montgomery, Alabama, where he responded to the arrest of activist Rosa Parks (who had refused to give up her seat on a city bus to a white passenger) by leading a successful boycott of the public transit system that lasted for 381 days.[26] In 1957 he established in Atlanta the Southern Christian Leadership Conference, a civil rights organization consisting largely of members of hundreds of southern black churches.[27] King's use of boycotts, sit-ins, marches, and protest rallies were designed to attract public attention to the injustices of the power structure and, through use of the public spotlight, invoke a sense of moral shame that would damage or diminish its prestige and economic standing. In response to his efforts, harassment and death threats against King and his family became commonplace. In 1958 King was stabbed in New York but survived. Meanwhile, acts of terrorism, including lynchings, mutilations, and bombings, were under way throughout the South. The white power structure maintained itself through not only the machinery of state governments and its various branches, but on a popular level through militant fraternal organizations, including Christian racialist groups such as the White League and the Ku Klux Klan. Undeterred by the pervasive threat of violence against himself and his supporters, King traveled to India in 1959 to further study Gandhi's teachings and strengthen his understanding of nonviolent resistance in his struggle to bring down the southern white system.

The 1960s marked a period of remarkable turmoil and activism in the United States, and King played a major role in those events. In 1960 he joined a lunch counter sit-in held in Montgomery, supporting the growing student demonstrations throughout the South against segregation. "Spontaneously born, but guided by the theory of nonviolence," he later wrote, "the lunch counter sit-ins accomplished integration in hundreds of communities at the swiftest rate of change in the civil rights movement up to that time."[28] King was arrested for sitting at a "whites only" lunch counter at a Rich's department store in Atlanta. In 1961 and 1962 he was arrested again, in Albany, Georgia, for working to desegregate public facilities. In April 1963 King was arrested in Birmingham, Alabama, where he wrote his famous jail-cell letter in response to a troubling public rebuke by local white Christian clergymen. "Just as Socrates felt that it was necessary to create a tension in the mind so that individuals could rise from the bondage of myths and half-truths to the unfettered realm of creative analysis and objective appraisal," he wrote, "so must we see the need for nonviolent gadflies to create the kind of tension in society that will help men rise from the dark depths of prejudice and racism to the majestic heights of understanding and brotherhood."[29]

In August 1963 King joined with other civil rights leaders and organizations to organize a massive march on the nation's capital, where he delivered his most famous speech, "I Have a Dream," standing before the Lincoln Memorial. The speech was delivered before a spellbound crowd of some 400,000 people and broadcast throughout the country by radio and television. It not only demonstrated King's superb oratory abilities, but elegantly articulated his ethical vision of racial equality in America as a fulfillment of its moral ideals and historical destiny. For many Americans, this moment reflected the pinnacle of his career and moral leadership.

There were, however, many critical years ahead. In 1964 King was awarded the Nobel Peace Prize for his nonviolent campaign against segregation and institutionalized racism in the United States. "I accept this award on behalf of a civil rights movement," he said, "which is moving with determination and a majestic scorn for risk and danger to establish a reign of freedom and a rule of justice." King further stated that the award was a "profound recognition that nonviolence is the answer to the crucial political and moral question of our time—the need for man to overcome oppression and violence without resorting to violence and oppression."[30] After President Lyndon B. Johnson signed the Voting Rights Act into law in 1965, King increasingly turned his attention to the problems of economic injustice in America and the Vietnam War. Focusing on these issues diminished his popularity and former base of support, especially among northern whites. But it never curbed his commitment to his ethical vision or zeal for justice. King referred to economic injustice as the "inseparable twin" of racial injustice. "Many white Americans of good will," he wrote, "have tolerated or ignored economic injustice."[31] As an expression of solidarity with the poor, King and his family moved into a Chicago slum, but he was unable to convince black youth of the utility of nonviolence. His marches in the summer of 1966 erupted into riots that King was unable to halt. Those marches that went through white neighborhoods in Chicago triggered attacks by white mobs, which King called worse than anything he had experienced in the South.[32]

On April 4, 1967, King gave a speech before an audience of three thousand people at New York City's Riverside Church. There he delivered one of the most forceful indictments ever made of America's Vietnam policies, calling the U.S. government "the greatest purveyor of violence in the world today."[33] The "madness of Vietnam," as King called it, was a damning indictment of America's power structure and its moral and ideological hypocrisy. "If America's soul becomes totally poisoned," he declared, "part of the autopsy must read 'Vietnam'."[34] Later that year, his estrangement from the Johnson administration grew when he announced the Poor People's Campaign. This controversial nonviolent campaign targeted the U.S. government directly by using sit-ins, demonstrations, and the building of a shantytown in Washington's government district.[35] King announced that he would lead a march on Washington to demand a massive multibillion dollar Economic Bill of Rights that guaranteed employment, incomes to those unable to work, and low-cost housing that would bring an end to housing discrimination.[36] "We're going to be militant," he said in reference to the nonviolent campaign. "We're going to plague Congress."[37] These years just prior to his assassination in April 1968 have been virtually erased from the American cultural narrative of his life and legacy. As a report from the organization Fairness and Accuracy in Reporting (FAIR) has noted, "national news media have never come to terms with what Martin Luther King Jr. stood for during his final years."[38]

Another prominent leader of nonviolent resistance was Mexican American labor leader and activist César Chávez, who worked to improve the working conditions of migrant farm workers in the American West, which he likened to slavery. His union, the United Farm Workers, utilized a range of nonviolent tactics, including strikes, boycotts, marches, and fasting, in its campaigns.[39] Chávez, however, differed from Gandhi and King as a leader of nonviolent resistance. His contributions were chiefly as an organizer and a man of action, rather than as an intellectual or philosopher of nonviolence. In an interview that he gave in 1973, Chávez explained:

> In our movement most of us are the action type and not the philosopher type. This is probably the most I'll ever do on nonviolence—talking when someone comes around and asks questions about it. I won't write about it. I don't want to write about it. I haven't got time. The philosophy is great, but you take Gandhi and King and learn from them because they were activists and strategists.[40]

Chávez worked to resist and defeat a political and economic power structure dominated by corporations run by white Americans that were exploiting previously disorganized and voiceless migrants, most of whom were Hispanic. The spirit of the resistance was perhaps best summarized by the words of an old American folk singer, Utah Phillips, who said, "You have to resist, because the profit system follows the path of least resistance, and following the path of least resistance is what makes the river crooked."[41]

Meanwhile, as Chávez was leading his campaigns in the United States, Archbishop Desmond Tutu was helping to lead a successful campaign of nonviolent resistance against the white power structure of apartheid South Africa. In the 1980s Desmond Tutu, an Anglican priest, was a leading advocate of international disinvestment in South Africa and one of the foremost international critics of the apartheid system. He was awarded the Nobel Peace Prize in 1984, where he declared, "In dehumanizing others, they are themselves dehumanized. Perhaps oppression dehumanizes the oppressor as much as, if not more than, the oppressed."[42] In 1990 the apartheid system in South Africa began to be dismantled, and discriminatory laws were gradually repealed. The international pressure and damage to South Africa's wealth and prestige by the activism of Tutu and others was too much for the white power structure to sustain. After serving in a reconciliation government elected in 1994, led by Nelson Mandela of the African National Congress (which had used violence against apartheid), Tutu turned to teaching, writing, and international activism, working particularly close with former U.S. president Jimmy Carter. In his efforts to promote peace throughout the world, Tutu has traveled to such conflict zones as the Palestinian territories, where he has worked with the Sabeel Ecumenical Liberation Theology Center founded by Rev. Naim Ateek in Jerusalem.

As described in chapter 1, the struggle between Arabs and Israelis in the Middle East has been dominated by a mind-numbing cycle of violence. However, several Christian and Muslim Palestinian activists, including Naim Ateek, Mubarak Awad, and Sari Nusseibeh, have worked to promote nonviolent resistance to the occupying Israeli power structure in the West Bank and Gaza. As Ateek has described it, the Israelis "know we are working for peace, and that we are a greater threat to them than Hamas, [because] Hamas allows them a pretext to continue the occupation—we do not."[43] For their efforts, these nonviolent activists have faced opposition on all sides. Nusseibeh, a Muslim with a PhD in Islamic philosophy from Harvard, has been beaten by militant Palestinian students, arrested by Israel, and gone into hiding from Islamist extremists. Awad, a Christian, was arrested by Israel in 1988 and deported to the United States where he now runs Nonviolence International and teaches at American University in Washington, D.C. Today destructive violence, built on an erroneous narrative of violence, remains the dominant mode of resistance throughout the West Bank and Gaza.

Many other names could have been included in this short historical narrative of nonviolence in the modern world. Choosing to exclude figures such as Dorothy Day, A. J. Muste, Thich Nhat Hanh, and Thomas Merton, among so many others, was not intended to diminish their contributions in any way. Rather, this brief history was only intended to provide readers with a brief look at the development of the modern concept of nonviolence as it relates to the analysis at hand. As for modern Muslim practitioners and philosophers of nonviolence, they will be the focus of subsequent chapters, and thus, except for Nusseibeh, they were deliberately excluded from this historical narrative as well.

Direct Action

At the onset of this chapter, we divided nonviolent strategies and tactics into two camps. Direct action, the first of the two, has been defined as the strategic use of immediately effective acts, such as strikes, demonstrations, or sabotage, to achieve a political or social end. Strategies and methods of direct action emphasize the importance of positive interdependence between the parties involved, which is increasingly easier to do in a globalized world. For example, if a power structure relies on the labor of a community in order to keep a society functioning, the community might also rely on the power structure for employment and land to produce food. The two factions are interdependent. However, those within the system may not have an appreciation or awareness of its dependence on the community. In such circumstances, the community will act to demonstrate that dependence by using such strategies as strikes, boycotts, and demonstrations. When the power structure no longer has the labor to maintain its economic interests and standard of living, it will ideally negotiate terms to have the community resume its labor. But such ideal situations are rare, and further long-term action campaigns are necessary in the majority of cases.

In circumstances where the power structure demonstrates a hostile unwilling-ness to reasonably address the discontent of the community, the "bread and circuses" that placate thousands or millions of people, lulling them into passivity and apathy, must be disrupted or removed. As American activist Mario Savio described in his famous 1964 speech on the steps of Sprout Hall at the University of California at Berkeley:

> There is a time when the operation of the machine becomes so odious, makes you so sick at heart, that you can't take part; you can't even passively take part, and you've got to put your bodies upon the gears and upon the wheels, upon the levers, upon all the apparatus, and you've got to make it stop.[44]

The "machine" that Savio described in his speech is a powerful metaphor for a range of power structures in the world today. As we already know, modern societies exist within political units called nation-states. Within those units, centralized governments (save for cases like Somalia) depend on their ability to make the societies and citizens that they govern "legible," in so far as they can be managed, organized, and, of course, taxed for revenue. Disrupting the instruments and mechanisms of governance through direct action is a powerful nonviolent strategy of resistance.

Gandhi employed a *hartal*, or general strike, as a demonstration of the vulnerability of the colonial state to the disruption of those functions. If a movement is large enough, as it was with Gandhi, a campaign may even include civil servants. Their refusal to perform the functions of the state can have a tremendous impact. For instance, a government that does not have sufficient obedience from its security forces to enforce its policies and laws on a community is incapable of bringing those policies or laws into being. Unjust laws become mere words without human beings to enforce them. But the community may not have the sympathy of the security forces either, which likely depend on income from the state power structure. The disruption of revenue channels (e.g., taxation and trade) can disrupt that government support.

Even thriving economies, such as that of the United States, remain deeply dependent on certain resources, such as fuel (specifically oil), to transport goods and run the automobiles that take the workforce to their place of business every day. Disruptions in the fuel supply, such as the 1973 Arab oil embargo, can have dramatic effects, even if they only raise the cost of fuel (which can cause a domino effect) for the mass citizenry. At a minimum such actions create growing discontent among the citizenry and criticism of the power structure's ability to govern. The privileges that the status quo or dominant social faction enjoy are challenged in light of increased economic difficulties and a declining standard of living among the majority of the people, resulting in a revolt of noncooperation. As Elizabeth Janeway noted in her essay *On the Power of the Weak*, "a withdrawal of attention, a lack of interest, a concentration on other areas, and finally, a turning to other prophets preaching other explanations of the world, are typical ways in which the weak exercise their power. . . . The absence of response frightens the powerful."[45]

Nonviolent direct action can target the image or perception of social control by disrupting political speeches, public ceremonies, and media events, as well as the overall public landscape. Media exposure, in such instances, is absolutely essential and undermines the dissemination of propaganda by the power structure. As nonviolent activist Tom Hastings has noted, nonviolent campaigns are most effective when they are able to "disrupt and delegitimize" the power structure's public relations.[46] This was certainly evident in the protest campaigns that utilized social media networks in Tunisia and Egypt during the "Arab Spring" of 2010 and 2011.

Related methods of direct action include subversive vandalism, art, music, and broadcast media. The cell-phone video of Neda Agha-Soltan's gruesome death, which I discuss in chapter 11, at the hands of security forces in Iran during the 2009 post-election protests did more damage to the Iranian power structure than any bomb or bullet. The protest folk songs and satirical poems of Swedish-American labor activist Joe Hill were considered so subversive to the exploitative capitalist power structure in the state of Utah that he was arrested and wrongly convicted (or framed) for murder and subsequently executed by firing squad in 1915. Since 1985 the masked feminist group Guerrilla Girls has challenged racial and gender discrimination and corruption in American culture through provocative works of art that have garnered worldwide attention to their causes and provoked social change.

A power structure, by its very nature, seeks to impose its decisions and images onto society and enforce conformity to those designs with minimal resistance, even in the area of aesthetics. At a minimum, subversive artistic expression disrupts the illusion of control and reveals a fundamental disconnect between the power structure and the human beings it seeks to control or exercise dominion over. For example, a government may officially disseminate propaganda expressing the utopian order of its society and the gracious contentment and loyalty of its people. But when the walls of buildings in that same society are covered with art and text that suggests otherwise, underground videos revealing atrocities and protests are circulated through the Internet, and the youth are chanting songs that ridicule the leader of the regime, the power structure and its legitimizing narratives are being delegitimized on a global scale. International outcries and diplomatic tensions ensue, focusing widespread attention on, and solidarity with, internal campaigns of nonviolent resistance, including the deaths of nonviolent activists.

Indirect Action

I am defining indirect action as the strategic use of nonviolent means to resist the power structure through long-term social and economic policies, including education and microfinance programs (discussed in detail in chapters 9 and 10). After all, there is a reason that discriminatory policies in the American South restricted education and employment opportunities for African Americans. Keeping them impoverished and uneducated remained in the interests of the white power structure trying to maintain its dominance. In Afghanistan, preventing girls from attending school and learning to read, or from working outside of the home, was in the interests of the patriarchal misogynistic hierarchy that the Taliban power structure sought to maintain. Education is an integral part of any successful nonviolent campaign; as the old saying goes, "knowledge is power." Or in the ancient words of the Prophet Muhammad, "The ink of a scholar's pen is holier than the blood of a martyr."

Proponents of violence, such as Islamist extremists, recognize the importance of schools, although they utilize them for indoctrination in the narrative of violence. Critical thinking and liberal thought are not educational objectives extremists tend to promote. After all, they believe that society can be transformed and glory attained simply through violence and bloodshed. Nonviolence proposes that the community acquire the necessary knowledge and skills to advance in society, thereby challenging the status quo of the power structure and provoking it in order to expose its unjust means and illegitimacy by seeking to prevent the advancement of the community. It is fundamentally the same strategy as a protest march but indirect and long term. For instance, the secular power structure in Turkey has attempted to prevent Muslim women from attending public universities while wearing a hijab, a traditional covering for the head and neck. This has been a public relations nightmare for the regime, however, as the secular power structure's claim that the country's Islamists oppose education and public life for women is being subverted by the government's own oppressive policy preventing women from completing their education. More broadly, however, the core strategy is really to equip members of the community with the necessary skills and knowledge to achieve success through nonviolent means. The narrative of violence will always be more attractive to an illiterate populace, because alternative avenues for social advancement are closed to them. Such a population may not be able to read or study at a university, but its members can pull a trigger or detonate a bomb as well as anyone.

The narrative of violence proposes that prosperity can be achieved by physically destroying the source of the community's discontent. However, economic opportunity will not only remain elusive once the violent elimination of the designated "source" is achieved, but it is highly likely that the necessary resources—infrastructure, roads, trade routes, and so on—will be destroyed in the process. Afghanistan provides a vivid example of this sad fact. In the ashes of its-once productive lands and thriving cities, war-torn Afghanistan remains a subsistence agrarian society where citizens must still avoid land mines in order to grow the only crop that seems to provide them with any reasonable income—opium poppies.

As was the case with education, the economic advancement of the community will challenge the power structure, causing it to expose its unjust means and illegitimacy by seeking to prevent the advancement of the community. One of the most exciting trends in the developing world over the past decades has been the emergence of microfinance institutions (MFIs). As described in greater detail in chapter 9, the Bangladeshi economist Muhammad Yunus is one of the pioneers of this important economic movement to eradicate poverty.

In 1983 Yunus established Grameen Bank (*grameen* means "village" in Bangla) in his native Bangladesh (one of the largest Muslim countries in the world), based on his study of impoverished female basket weavers in the village of Jobra in 1976. He recognized that the banks refused to provide loans to the poor and forced them to rely on dangerous money lenders who imposed exploitative interest rates, perpetuating an "age-old vicious circle of 'low income, low saving and low investment.'"[47] Since that time, Yunus's microfinance programs have spread to countries around the world and inspired other similar programs. In 2006 Yunus and Grameen Bank were awarded the Nobel Peace Prize. The Norwegian Nobel Committee's announcement stated, "Lasting peace cannot be achieved unless large population groups find ways in which to break out of poverty." The committee further stated that microfinancing "has proved to be an important liberating force in societies where women in particular have to struggle against repressive social and economic conditions."[48]

Among the other leading microfinance programs in the developing world is Foundation for International Community Assistance (FINCA). FINCA's emphasis on women reflects the disturbing fact that "seventy percent of the world's poor are women, largely because of their limited access to education or to productive resources like land and credit."[49] In 1984 American economist John Hatch created a microloan program for low-income farmers in Bolivia that allowed them to obtain loans without collateral (their main obstacle to accessing credit) at interest rates that they could afford. Hatch's "village banking" program gave community members the power to collectively disburse, invest, and collect loan capital as they saw fit. In the 1990s FINCA extended its programs into the Muslim world beginning with Kyrgyzstan, followed by Azerbaijan, Kosovo, and Tajikistan. In 2003 FINCA began work in Afghanistan, and five years later it was in Jordan. By operating in Muslim societies, especially conservative Middle Eastern societies, FINCA and other MFIs have reconciled their methods with the prohibition against usury in Islamic law. The "loan" that FINCA offers in Afghanistan and Jordan is "a pre-approved and mutually agreed upon sale contract that explicitly itemizes the sale of a commodity for cash plus a markup, including administrative costs associated with the transaction."[50]

The impact of microfinancing administered by Grameen Bank, FINCA, and other MFIs is far greater than simply improved economic growth in Muslim societies. These programs can ultimately break the dependence of these communities on existing power structures by allowing them to help themselves, which is a tremendous source of personal empowerment. They can furthermore facilitate improvement in general health and education, because the loans, especially to women, allow children to have greater access to nutritious food and essential schooling.

The narrative of violence will always be more attractive to an illiterate person because alternative avenues for social advancement are closed to them. Given the disturbing emergence of child soldiers in the developing world, providing opportunities for children to build productive lives is more important than ever. The cultivation of the mind and body through education and healthy lifestyles is essential to the success of nonviolent resistance. For example, fasting is a common tactic employed in campaigns of nonviolent resistance, but it is certainly ill-advised if community members are already suffering from malnutrition and starvation. Nonviolent activists must possess the ability to physically and psychologically sustain the abuse and violence that may be enacted on them by agents of the oppressive system to the best of their abilities, even though death may still be the end result.

The Physiology of Rage

Intense anger or rage is a serious obstacle to the successful enactment of nonviolence by participants engaged in a campaign of resistance. The history of modern nonviolence has shown that power structures will resort to the most brutal forms of violence to disrupt campaigns of resistance against their dominance. In some cases it is the goal of the oppressor to provoke its opponents into violence. It is quite natural for participants to struggle with feelings of anger as they are harassed, abused, brutalized, or worse by the agents of the power structure.

Previously I referred to the need for discipline and courage among successful practitioners of nonviolence. But, in doing so, practitioners will have to grapple with traits hardwired into the human brain. In 1872 Charles Darwin produced a treatise in which he noted that anger and aggression have survival value in warding off danger, or what we might commonly call the fight-or-flight response.[51] Some scholars, such as Oliver Goodenough of Harvard University, have recently argued that "genetics and brain chemicals can conspire to severely limit a person's ability to choose a nonviolent solution to a situation."[52] Still other scholars have found that the human brain seeks violence in the same way it seeks food or sex. Craig Kennedy of Vanderbilt University has stated that aggression "serves a really useful evolutionary role . . . which is you defend territory; you defend your mate; if you're a female, you defend your offspring."[53] There is obviously a greater challenge inherent in resisting the urge to commit acts of violence than one might ordinarily realize.

We know that the brain craves food and that the human body has a strong physiological response to the need for food. The response of the body is perfectly understandable because we obviously need food to survive. But human beings are still capable of fasting and resisting the powerful urge to eat. Muslims practice a thirty-day fast, abstaining from food and water, during the sacred month of Ramadan every year. For a devout Jain who has reached the end of his or her life, the most noble form of death is a voluntary fast. This act is called *santhara*, and it was reportedly practiced by Vardhamana himself in the fifth century BCE. The same discipline involved in fasting and other ascetic practices can obviously be applied to any intrinsic human inclinations toward violence.

Scientists have found that anger causes a range of physiological processes in the brain and body that impact our behavior and choice of action. Anger has been found to restrict the amount of oxygen that reaches the brain because the physiological response causes tension throughout the body that restricts circulation, as well as the release of clotting agents into the bloodstream. This results in impaired thinking, decreasing the ability of the brain to rationally cope with a situation. Such instances could be described as "blind rage." Given this fact, breathing techniques commonly employed in various forms of meditation, including yoga, could provide helpful assistance in the enactment of nonviolent resistance. In addition, as strange as it may sound, laughter has also been shown to help the body and brain alleviate impairment and other negative effects brought on by feelings of anger. A healthy dose of humorous ridicule aimed at the power structure in nonviolent campaigns may go a long way toward benefiting the success of such efforts.

The Problem of Genocide

In his influential nineteenth-century treatise *On War*, Carl von Clausewitz defined "war" as a large-scale "act of violence to compel our enemy to do our will." But what if the intent of a war is not to compel the enemy to do our will, but to eliminate the enemy's very existence from the planet? The problem of genocide is critical and exposes the practical limits of nonviolence. As Hannah Arendt noted, "if Gandhi's enormously powerful and successful strategy of nonviolent resistance had met with a different enemy, [such as] Stalin's Russia, Hitler's Germany, even prewar Japan, instead of England, the outcome would not have been decolonization, but massacre and submission."[54]

When confronted by genocide, the narrative of nonviolence becomes displaced. A new narrative emerges in its stead that is fundamentally dissimilar. This new narrative is one of survival, and it is no longer concerned with the power, prosperity, and prestige of the community. The narrative of survival is concerned with the preservation of the community in the face of total eradication. As Arendt noted, nonviolence would have been an ineffective strategy to be employed by victims such as the Muslims of Bosnia, the Hutus of Rwanda, or the Jews of Germany. Nonviolence is a powerful strategy to resist oppression, control, and injustice, but it cannot resist the systematic annihilation of an entire population. There are a few proponents of nonviolence who would disagree with this assertion, but such views are radically idealistic and untenable. That said, there may be *preemptive* nonviolent measures that can prevent the implementation of genocide before it occurs.

One of the most telling precursors to genocide is a shift in the language of the public discourse. Genocide operates through the narrative of violence by "Othering" a particular racial, ethnic, or religious group, or even a particular sexual orientation, and branding that Other as the source of the community's discontent that must be defeated or eliminated for prosperity to occur. If the discourse fails to successfully Other a particular group and convincingly connect that group to the discontent of the community, genocide will not be manifested, even if acts of violence are. In that case nonviolent resistance becomes tenable again. But if the rhetoric of "Otherness" is not disrupted and it succeeds, then genocide can be enacted because human actors will no longer be restrained by any sense of injustice or moral shame, since the target of their violence is fundamentally unlike "them" and not worthy of empathy or compassion. The Jew was "fundamentally unlike" the Aryan in Nazi Germany, right down to "its" hair and bones. Even so, the perpetrators of genocide typically try to hide their atrocities from the outside world, because even if their victims cannot evoke a sense of moral shame, world-wide condemnation and rebuke can still succeed in doing so. At the very least, it can destroy their international standing and economic ties in the world. New media, such as online videos or digital recordings, can be a useful tool in expos-ing potentially genocidal rhetoric and behavior to the outside world, and it can be disseminated freely and almost instantaneously around the world. Readers will recall that in the mid-twentieth century, the international community expressed the upsetting excuse that "we did not know what was going on" under the Third Reich. This is an ever increasing impossibility in the twenty-first century, where privacy from the media is ever more elusive.

Toward Islamic Nonviolence

The champions of nonviolence that I discussed in this chapter come from many backgrounds and nationalities. Most readers are already familiar with these figures, especially Mohandas K. Gandhi and Martin Luther King Jr. It is also likely that many readers do not have any knowledge or awareness of Muslim champions of nonviolence. Readers might even express skepticism that Islamic nonviolence is possible given the outrageous violence that afflicts the contemporary Muslim world. Rest assured, however, that Islamic nonviolence is very much a reality and that its champions are numerous.

Over the ensuing chapters of this book, I will introduce you to several of the most prominent champions of nonviolence in the modern Muslim world. These inspiring people come from many different countries and schools of thought, yet they all see nonviolence as something that is fully compatible with the Qur'an and the teachings of the Prophet Muhammad. By examining these figures and their interpretations of Islam, it is my hope that non-Muslim readers will better appreciate the rich diversity and peaceful aspects of Islam, and that Muslim readers will better appreciate the important heritage that their brothers and sisters in Islam have left them for the future.

4

The Chieftain

Our look at the Muslim champions of nonviolence begins with a most extraordinary one. Abdul Ghaffar Khan, known to his people as Badshah Khan, is a fascinating figure little known outside of the Indian subcontinent. As an ethnic Pashtun (or Pakhtun) from the tribes of the Indus River Valley, where cool waters converge from the grand mountains of Tibet, Khan existed in a world rife with divisive tribal violence and constant threats of foreign conquest. That one of the greatest champions of nonviolence emerged from such a troubled place has always seemed remarkable to me.

The Pashtuns were an ancient nation of fierce and rugged warriors, known to carry daggers or rifles as everyday wear, who were governed by an ancient tribal code, known as *Pashtunwali*. Feuds over *zar*, *zan*, and *zamin*—gold, women, and land—were commonplace and marred daily life.[1] Legends among the neighboring peoples even claimed (erroneously) that the Pashtuns drank the blood of their enemies! As Khan reached adulthood, the lands of the fierce Pashtuns, between the Hindu Kush (home to the strategically vital geographic passageway known as the Khyber Pass) and the Indus River became a major center of violent revolt and agitation against foreign occupation by the British Empire. To preserve their colonial domains, the British carried out brutal troop sweeps, shellings, air raids, floggings, and arrests to subdue the troublesome Pashtun tribes in the North-West Frontier Province (often referred to as "the Frontier"). Ironically, the army of nonviolence raised by Khan proved to be the most formidable foe for the British Empire in the whole of the subcontinent.

The Early Years

Legend says that the Pashtuns are the descendents of the Israelite king Saul, tracing their lineage to the far-off tribes of the Holy Land. But the man later known as Badshah Khan was born in a simple farming village called Utmanzai, now in northwestern Pakistan, near the city of Peshawar in 1890 (although the exact date is unknown). His father, Bahram Khan, was a landowner and a village chief from the Mohammedzai clan, said to descend from the Prophet Muhammad. Bahram was a very well-respected and trusted chieftain known for his modesty, hospitality, and support for education among his people. In his autobiography, Khan described his father as "extremely even-tempered, God-fearing, sober, generous, compassionate, and of noble character."[2] Bahram was a devout Sunni Muslim, known to keep his five daily prayers, and well known for his dislike of feuds or vendettas—strangely, at least for a Pashtun chieftain, preferring forgiveness over revenge. As one nineteenth-century European observer noted, describing the traditional Pashtun concept of *badal* (vendetta), "revenge is a word sweet to the Pathan ear."[3] Bahram Khan passed his progressive views, including his dislike of senseless violence, onto his children, including his youngest son, Abdul Ghaffar.

As a boy Khan began his schooling in the madrassa of a local mosque, learning the most rudimentary elements of Islam and how to read the Arabic script of the sacred Qur'an. There were very few government schools in the area—unlike the rest of British India—and their teachers were not Pashtuns, nor did they teach children in their native language, Pashto.[4] The task of educating Pashtun children was thus left largely to conservative and abusive clerics, or mullahs. Keen to protect their positions, the mullahs regularly denounced anyone who sent their children to the British schools as "infidels."[5] The mullahs were woefully incompetent but enjoyed a social standing rooted in the Pashtun culture. Khan later described his own cruel teacher as "practically illiterate" and unqualified to even teach him the alphabet.[6] Nevertheless, he excelled in his studies and memorized the entirety of the Qur'an, an achievement that delighted his mother and father. There are numerous prophetic traditions in the revered hadith collections of Abu Dawud, Tirmidhi, Bukhari, and others that extol the heavenly rewards that God bestows on someone who memorizes the Qur'an—even a single verse.

When Khan was eight years old, his father sent him to follow his older brother and attend a primary school, despite the condemnation of the local mullahs. "Fortunately for me God had blessed me with a brave and broad-minded father and a saintly and loving mother," he recalled, "both of whom ignored the mullahs' condemnation and took no notice of what the neighbors said."[7] The school that he attended was located in the nearby city of Peshawar. Little did he know at the time, but the Pashtun people and the British were rapidly moving on a collision course that would forever alter his future.

In 1901, the year that King Edward VII ascended to the throne, the British Empire enacted the Frontier Crimes Regulation (FCR) to allow the arrest and transport of any troublesome Pashtun without counsel or trial, creating a cruel police state of collective hardship. The British, Khan later wrote, "introduced new and brutal laws to our province, laws not even Hulagu Khan [the Mongol warlord] would have enforced on the people."[8] The FCR came to be ominously known among the Pashtuns as the "black law." Under it authorities could "start a fictitious case against anyone the British happened to dislike" without proof or evidence, and it was commonly used to imprison Pashtun political prisoners.[9] "This uncivilized act," wrote Khan, "did great damage to our self-respect and honor."[10] Honor is dear to the Pashtun heart—even more so than life itself.

Khan now studied at a school run by Anglican missionaries, while his older brother, Abdul Jabbar (later known as Dr. Khan Sahib), left to study medicine in Mumbai. The missionary school was a positive experience for the bright, young Abdul Ghaffar. His headmaster at the school was Rev. E. F. E. Wigram, an Anglican priest of the Church Missionary Society educated in the prestigious halls of Cambridge University. Wigram had a significant influence on his young Pashtun student from Utmanzai. Decades later Khan would still recall how Wigram's devotion to serving the poor and the needy, regardless of nationality or religion, greatly impressed him. "There is a Persian proverb [that] when a melon sees another melon, it takes on its color," he recalled, "so, the color of service and dedication that I saw in Mr. Wigram and his brother [a doctor at the mission hospital], must have fallen on me too."[11] His early experiences among the British had not yet swayed him to join the struggle against them as occupiers, but things would quickly change.

At the mission school, Khan heard stories about an elite British Army unit called the Guides. It was one of the few positions open to non-Englishmen. A friend of Khan's had joined and spoke often about life in the Guides as glamorous and a way to earn respect among the English. Intrigued, Khan applied for a direct commission, and much to his delight it was granted. "Admission into [the Guides unit] was not easy," he later wrote, "and even rich and influential families found it difficult to get their sons enlisted in this regiment."[12] His adulation ended when he witnessed his friend, a cavalry officer, being publicly ridiculed by an English lieutenant on the streets of Peshawar. Looking at his friend's European style of haircut, the lieutenant shouted, "You damn Sardar Saheb! So you want to be an Englishman, do you?"[13] The incident left a deep impression on Khan, and he saw it as a "gross and despicable insult." This was no small matter for a Pashtun, as according to Pashtunwali any insult or attack on the honor, people, or property of a tribesman demanded badal, which had no time limit and could last for generations. On that very day, Khan gave up the idea of joining the British Army. "It did not give one any respect," he later wrote. "In fact, it made one a slave and one risked being insulted in the bargain."[14] Khan's father was angry with his rash decision, but his brother, at a medical college in London at the time, wrote in support of Khan and implored Bahram not to force him into service. He relented and accepted his son's decision.

A New Direction

With the army out of the picture, Khan returned to his studies. But when he went home for holiday break, he learned that a letter had arrived from his brother urging Bahram to send him to London to study engineering. His father approved, but Khan's mother simply refused to allow her second son to join his brother overseas. Tears flowed. She worried that her sons would never return and no one would care for her in her old age. Always devoted to his mother, Khan agreed to stay. "So I gave up the idea of going abroad," he later wrote, "and decided that henceforth I would devote myself to the service of my country and my people, the service of God and humanity."[15]

Khan set to work in the farmlands of the village, where he observed the distressing conditions of his people. Most had no education. They knew nothing of the world beyond their daily subsistence. Seeing them plagued by violence and injustice, he set out to create a series of social and religious reforms. But the mullahs, backed by the British Raj, were intent on preventing any such progress and preserving their own authority in the villages, which included the extraction of alms. These mullahs were incorrigibly stubborn, and, in Khan's view, they were "puppets in the hands of the British."[16] Yet he was no longer a frightened school-boy, but an educated man of great size (6 feet, 3 inches tall and over two hundred pounds), well-versed in Islam. He refuted the mullahs' objections and attempted to persuade them by citing Islam's emphasis on the acquisition of knowledge, especially the ability to read. "By all means tell people not to send their children to British schools," he said to them, "but then also tell them to build schools of their own where their children can be educated [as] a service to the country."[17] The stubborn mullahs would not listen, so Khan decided to take responsibility for the endeavor himself. His first task was eliminating illiteracy.[18]

Khan and a circle of friends established a school in Gadar in 1910. A second school soon followed in Utmanzai. More came after them, and Pashtun enrollment grew rapidly, as did interest in education and the outside world. Khan also established ties with the Darul-Ulum madrassa at Deoband. Founded in 1864, it was built as a center for the revival of Islam and the elimination of any accretions seen as a source of Islam's decline. But Deoband also offered a modern educational system that reflected the early twentieth-century colonial atmosphere of northern India. It relied on public support, rather than government funds. And this gave the school the respectability of political independence.

Deobandis were generally conservative and hardly averse to notions of military jihad against the British. Khan, however, shared their interest in the advancement of Muslim peoples through education. Shaykh ul-Hind Mehmud ul-Hasan and Obaidullah Sindhi were two of the leading Deobandi scholars he worked with.[19] Both advocated pan-Islamic ideals, in line with the late Jamal al-Din al-Afghani, that supported the institutional symbol of Muslim solidarity, the Ottoman Caliphate in Istanbul. The outbreak of World War I in 1914 threatened the future of the Ottoman Empire and the sanctity of the Muslim holy places, including Jerusalem, which fell under British control. The entire Muslim world, it seemed, was on the verge of humiliating subjugation to the European colonial powers.

The outcome of the war brought increased urgency to Khan's efforts. Looking for allies, he began to work with the Khilafat Movement. The Khilafat Movement started in 1919 as an effort to save the Caliphate and the Ottoman Empire from the European powers after the war.[20] Among their early positions, the Khilafatists advocated migration from British India to Afghanistan to create a free Muslim state and to organize anti-British campaigns. Obaidullah Sindhi was among the Indian Muslim leaders who migrated to Kabul, the royal capital of Afghanistan. Khan, however, remained behind.

Since the start of the war, Khan had worked with growing numbers of volunteers, traveling by foot from village to village (some five hundred in all), teaching and establishing schools, and advocating an end to badal. And much to the villagers' shock, he did not accept alms from them like the mullahs used to do. The people adored him and were so impressed by his message that they bestowed on Abdul Ghaffar Khan the name Badshah Khan, meaning "King of the Khans [chieftains]." Thereafter, whenever he entered a village he was met with the joyous cry "Badshah Khan is coming!"[21] Meanwhile, the British imposed new restrictions and cracked down on any dissent during the war. Schools were closed or demolished, newspapers were censored or banned, political meetings were curtailed, and secret military tribunals filled the prisons with people longing for freedom.[22]

The British won Indian support during the war with vague promises of greater freedoms, but when the war ended, the Rowlatt Act kept wartime restrictions in place. Across the subcontinent, people were enraged. At the start of the war, Mohandas Gandhi had returned from South Africa, adopted an ascetic lifestyle, and began promoting nonviolent resistance to British rule. He gave public speeches and produced publications, and he emerged as a leader of the Indian National Congress. Gandhi was fiercely opposed to the Rowlatt Act and called for a nationwide day of protest, creating a hartal in which all shops and businesses shut down. Khan answered Gandhi's call and organized a protest of over 100,000 people in Utmanzai that energized the Pashtuns to resist British tyranny.[23]

Shaken, the British declared martial law. Khan and his supporters went into hiding but were soon discovered, arrested, and transported in chains to Peshawar. "The fetters they had put on me were so tight that I could hardly walk," he later recalled. "The skin was rubbed off my feet and they were bleeding."[24] Rumors were spread that Khan had been hanged, and the British looted Utmanzai, terrorized and fined its people, and imprisoned many others, including his father. Even so, the people would not give up their struggle. Six months passed before Khan was released from his lice-infested cell. None of his fellow Pashtuns would testify against him in court, despite British attempts to bribe the impoverished tribesmen.

Khan's first wife, the mother of his two young sons, had died tragically from influenza in 1918. Still a young man, despite the burden on his shoulders, he happily remarried in 1920 in a traditional arrangement made by his parents. This was the time when the Khilafatists had suggested that all Muslims in India migrate to Afghanistan. Concerned for the future of his young family, Khan traveled to Kabul, where he met with King Amanullah and toured schools. To his dismay, the students could not speak their own language, Pashto, and conversed in Dari (Persian). He boldly asked the Afghan minister of foreign affairs, "What I want to know is why you people have forgotten your own language?"[25] Troubled, Khan returned home disappointed. Preserving his nation's language was part of the resistance, and he would now devote himself to its survival.

At a meeting of the pro-independence Indian National Congress in Nagpur, Khan and the other attendees agreed to stay in India and fight nonviolently for freedom. Gandhi addressed the meeting and impressed Khan and many others with his calmness in the face of opposition. The independence movement against the British was gaining momentum fast. Later that year, Khan's brother, Dr. Khan Sahib, returned home after fifteen years in England completing his medical studies. The sons of Bahram Khan were happily reunited.

In 1921 Badshah Khan established Azad High School in Utmanzai, which taught students in their mother tongue, Pashto. This was an integral part of preserving the identity of his people. The British disapproved, however, and subjected the staff and students to threats and harassment. In some cases the British tried to lure teachers away with promises of better-paying jobs elsewhere.[26] The British chief commissioner, Sir John Maffey, even summoned Bahram Khan to his office in Peshawar to ask him to curtail the efforts of his son. Bahram agreed and returned to ask Badshah Khan to simply live a quiet family life. But Badshah Khan, upset by his father's rebuke, responded:

"Father, if everybody else stopped saying their daily prayers, would you advise me to do the same?" My father replied: "God forbid! Saying *namaz* is a sacred duty." I said: "And to my mind educating the people and serving the nation is as sacred a duty as prayer."[27]

The argument won his father over. Bahram Khan sent word to the chief commissioner that his son's efforts would not cease. The British would not relent though, and Badshah Khan was arrested. Sentenced to three years in solitary confinement, he endured terrible conditions unsuitable even for an animal. His brother later came to visit and deliver a message from the government. The British would free him, Khan Sahib said, if Badshah Khan would stop traveling to the villages. Badshah Khan refused. He could not be bribed to betray his beliefs. He even refused to bribe his jailor, as many other prisoners did, to avoid hard labor or other difficulties.

Transported from prison and released at Utmanzai in 1924, Khan was enthusiastically welcomed back by the villagers. The people even gave him a new honorary title, Fakhr-e Afghan, meaning the "Pride of the Afghans."[28] He found that the school had made good progress in his absence. However, away from Utmanzai, Mustafa Kemal Atatürk's abolition of the Caliphate in Turkey shocked Khan's peers in the Khilafat Movement. If the British had abolished the Caliphate, the Khilafatists would have had a compelling grievance against them to rally Indian Muslim unity in cooperation with Indian nationalism.[29] Instead, it was the leader of the Turks, the father of the new Turkish republic, who had done the unthinkable. Rival candidates to revive the Caliphate emerged in Arabia, but disputes among the Khilafatists foiled the future of the movement. The age of the Muslim empires had officially come to a close. Nationalism was sweeping the world.

Collision Course

In 1926, Khan's father died. Alms traditionally distributed to the mullahs after the death of a Pashtun tribesman were given instead to the school at Utmanzai. The two brothers were now the leaders of the village. Badshah Khan and his wife joined his sister on the hajj to Mecca that year, traveling by steamboat from Karachi to Jeddah. The great pilgrimage is a time of spiritual rebirth, and people seldom return from the hajj the same as when they left. The hajj that year also happened to coincide with an international Islamic conference in Mecca. Khan, as well as leaders of the Khilafat movement, attended. It proved a disappointment, though, as he would later write, "No problem of any importance was discussed and instead of promoting harmony the conference ended in discord."[30] Those leaders had no solutions to the problems that plagued the Muslims. Khan would have to do things his own way.

In the stark, sun-drenched deserts of Arabia, Khan traveled to the mountain city of Taif, north of Mecca, where conditions are more temperate and provide a refuge from the heat. Taif was an important city during the Prophet Muhammad's lifetime and a center of worship for one of several pagan goddesses. The Prophet had preached his message of monotheism and moral accountability at Taif in 620. But the people there sent out their slaves and children to stone the Prophet in the streets. Tradition relates that he was bloodied, badly injured, and nearly killed. When Khan visited Taif, a bearded man dressed in long traditional robes called him over on the street. The man quietly asked if he would like to see some relics of the Prophet, including a hair from his beard and his footprint in a stone. Khan immediately objected and replied:

> I have not come here to see relics. I have come here to look for the patience and courage of the Holy Prophet, who braved the journey through the desert from Mecca and came here for the welfare of the people of Taif. And how did the people of Taif receive him? They threw stones at him, set their dogs at him and beat him. But in spite of this cruelty the Prophet did not despair of the people, but he prayed for them, saying: "Oh God, be Thou their Guide and show them Thy ways."[31]

The man had no reply. He was awestruck by the curious, towering Pashtun. He was unlike the other pilgrims. From Taif, Khan traveled back to the holy cities of Mecca and Medina, riding a camel in the coolness of the night through the desert. "All around us was desert, silence, and peace," he later wrote. From Medina, they traveled to Jerusalem, where the sacred al-Aqsa Mosque sits next to the shimmering gold Dome of the Rock, marking the place where the Prophet ascended through the heavens. But tragedy struck in the holy city when Khan's wife fell from a staircase and died. "Losing my life's companion so suddenly was a terrible shock to me," he recalled. "I never married again, though I was still a young man."[32]

Khan continued his travels alone through Palestine, visiting the Muslim shrines and sacred places that dot the rugged landscape. From Palestine he went to Lebanon, Syria, and Iraq. He visited the sacred cities of Najaf and Karbala, revered among the Shi'ite Muslims, and finally Baghdad, Basra, and again to Karachi. A steamboat carried him on the last leg of his journey to Utmanzai, where he still had children to raise. He was no longer the same man that had left the Frontier so many months ago. He saw a Muslim renaissance of sorts and became keenly aware of the nationalism emerging in other countries that looked to India for inspiration. "India was the cornerstone of the British Empire; if that stone were removed, British power in the Middle East might topple, and that of the French could follow."[33] His struggle was no longer simply for India, but for all Muslims living under occupation.

After his return, Khan established a Pashto journal, *Pakhtun*. Literature in Pashto was virtually nonexistent. "A nation is known and recognized by its language," Khan later wrote, "and without a language of its own a nation cannot really be called a nation."[34] It rapidly grew in popularity and reached Pashtuns around the world. American Pashtuns financially supported the journal's publication and dissemination.[35] The success inspired a new Pashto journal in neighboring Afghanistan as well, called *Jagh Pakhtun*, under the auspices of King Amanullah. Soon all Afghan government employees had to learn Pashto. For this seemingly innocuous act, Khan later wrote, the British fomented revolt against the Afghan king and forced him to retreat into exile in Italy.

In 1928 Khan went to Lucknow for a meeting of the Indian National Congress. There he met with Gandhi and Jawaharlal Nehru for the first time. His brother had studied with Nehru in England, and Khan presented a letter of introduction.[36] They discussed much at their meeting, including conditions in Afghanistan. Badshah Khan had found new allies in his struggle for freedom.

After Lucknow, Khan traveled to a Khilafat conference in Calcutta, the crowded cultural capital of India. The Khilafatists had been substantially weakened since the end of the Caliphate. Nevertheless, they still promoted Muslim interests, especially in the independence movement. Khan's commitment to the Khilafatists was wavering when he arrived and did not survive their meeting. He witnessed the gathering in Calcutta devolve into a shocking exchange of insults and even violence. Khan spoke privately to the leaders to advise restraint and greater tolerance, as Gandhi had shown in contentious meetings, but he was dismissed as a mere Pashtun who had no right to teach anyone about restraint or tolerance. Khan severed his ties to the Khilafatists and thereafter increased his association with Gandhi and the Indian National Congress.

In the winter of 1929, Khan established a new Muslim organization, the Khudai Khidmatgars, or "the Servants of God." He had seen how the Pashtun villagers were disorganized and lacked devotion to national service. The new organization would bring them into the heart of the nationalist struggle for independence. Inspired by his studies of Islam and interaction with Gandhi, Khan decided that the Pashtuns would form an army for freedom but one devoted to nonviolence—the first nonviolent army in history. Each member took the same oath with a hand on the Qur'an, stating, "I am a Servant of God, and as God needs no service, but serving His creation is serving Him, I promise to serve humanity in the name of God; I refrain from violence and from taking revenge, I promise to forgive those who oppress me or treat me with cruelty."[37] The Khidmatgars were thereafter organized into military units, complete with ranks and uniforms. The clothing they wore was initially white, but as they traveled the countryside the dirt from the roads would sully them, so they took to dyeing their uniforms red by using a solution meant to tan animal hides. Due to their appearance, the British commonly referred to the Khidmatgars as the "Red Shirts."

The establishment of the Khudai Khidmatgars was arguably the greatest implementation of Islamic nonviolence in modern history. The level of activism was unique among the figures profiled in this book. The fact that it consisted of fearsome Pashtun warriors makes it all the more unique. In fact, it was argued by Gandhi and others that the warrior culture of the Pashtuns made them especially suitable for the implementation of nonviolence. Nevertheless, persuading the tribesmen to put down their bloodstained weapons was a challenge. Khan often spoke of the violence that plagued the Pashtuns, stating, "They were like smoldering embers, always ready to flare up and inflict harm and injury on their own brethren."[38] To convince them, he used the grassroots strategy employed in his education campaigns. "We went from village to village, talked to the people, founded *jirgas* [assemblies of elders], and enlisted *Khudai Khidmatgars* in all parts of the province . . . and soon it became so popular that *jirgas* and *Khudai Khidmatgars* were established in every village we visited."[39]

In time, the Khidmatgars grew to over 100,000 members. The British began to attend Khan's meetings, too, and marveled at his ability to enlist the Pashtuns for his cause. Many chieftains were puzzled by his talk of nonviolence, though. After all, the Prophet Muhammad had fought battles, and the jihad of the sword was practiced widely by Islamic kingdoms, including those in Afghanistan. Khan replied that there was nothing new about Islamic nonviolence, asserting that the Prophet had practiced it thirteen hundred years ago in Mecca.

The Meccan period (610–622) of the Prophet's life began with the first revelation of the Qur'an when he was meditating in a cave on Mount Hira. Eighty-five of the Qur'an's 114 suras date from this period. Unlike during the Medinan period, dating from 622 to 632, the idea of a military jihad did not yet exist. For perspective, we should recall that the ministry of Jesus of Nazareth lasted no more than three years. But Muhammad survived the persecution and assassination attempts at Mecca. He and his followers fled to the city of Yathrib, now known as Medina. This event is known as the *hijra* and marks year one of the Islamic calendar. In Medina the Prophet became the chief of the city, or "head of state," responsible for the city's welfare. The revelations received from Allah in Medina therefore involved greater sociopolitical interests, including warfare. All of the verses on warfare in the Qur'an are found in the Medinan suras, reflecting the difficult conditions of the time.

In his teachings, Khan emphasized Muhammad's Meccan period, as well as the lives of Muslim saints and sages who emulated the Prophet's conduct. To make his message plain, Khan believed that Islam could be summarized by three key concepts—namely, *amal, yakeen,* and *muhabat* ("work," "faith," and "love")—and said that "without these the name Muslim is sounding brass and tinkling cymbal."[40] He saw these concepts manifested in the life of the Prophet. He even called Islamic nonviolent resistance the "weapon of the Prophet," stating:

I am going to give you such a weapon that the police and the army will not be able to stand against it. It is the weapon of the Prophet, but you are not aware of it. That weapon is patience and righteousness. No power on earth can stand against it. When you go back to your villages, tell your brethren there is an army of God and its weapon is patience. Ask your brethren to join the army of God. Endure all hardships. If you exercise patience, victory will be yours.[41]

In the Meccan suras of the Qur'an, specifically *Surat al-Shura*, there is an important passage regarding violence and the rights of retaliation. Such passages can certainly support nonviolence:

The recompense for an injury is an injury equal thereto, but if a person forgives and makes reconciliation, his reward is due from God, for God loves not those who do wrong. But indeed if any do help and defend themselves after a wrong is done to them, against such a person there is no cause for blame. The blame is only against those who oppress others with wrongdoing and insolently transgress beyond bounds throughout the land, defying right and justice. For such people there will be a terrible penalty. But indeed if any one of you show patience and forgive, that would truly be an exercise of courageous will and resolution in the conduct of affairs.[42]

To summarize, the Qur'an forbids aggression but permits Muslims to retaliate in self-defense in equal measure ("an eye for an eye"). There is no sin in doing so, but it is important to note that there is no *reward* for doing so either. The reward from God, as the passage states, belongs to those who show patience and forgive—the superior path of the righteous believers—rather than those who retaliate with violence. Indeed, the Qur'an elsewhere advises Muslims to "respond to evil with what is good, and your enemy will become like a close and affectionate friend, but only those who are steadfast in patience, only those who are blessed with great righteousness, will attain such goodness."[43]

After three months, the British would take no more. They ordered Khan to cease his activities, but he refused. After a large meeting of Khudai Khidmatgars

in Utmanzai, Khan was arrested on his way to Peshawar. The arrest had an unexpected consequence, however. He was taken into custody at Naki Thana (on
the outskirts of Peshawar), which had no Khudai Khidmatgars at that time. The
people were so insulted and enraged by Khan's arrest that they all—Muslims,
Sikhs, and Hindus—joined together and decried the tyranny of British rule.

On April 23, British troops stormed the town to suppress the uprising, resulting in what is known as the Qissa Khawani Bazaar massacre, a defining moment
in the struggle for independence. British troops killed hundreds of unarmed dem-
onstrators over a span of several hours, mostly with gunfire (some were run over)
aimed at human walls of Muslims, as well as Sikhs and Hindus, standing arm
in arm. "The police opened fire and a number of people fell as martyrs for our
cause," Khan recalled understatedly.[44] As many as four hundred unarmed Khudai
Khidmatgars, clutching the Qur'an and chanting "God is great," were slaughtered on that day, and many others were wounded.[45] One scholar described the
events: "When those in front fell down wounded by the shots, those behind came
forward with their chests bared and exposed themselves to the fire, so much so
that some people got as many as twenty-one bullet wounds in their bodies, and all
the people stood their ground without getting into a panic."[46] The carnage reportedly went on for six hours. When news of it spread throughout the subcontinent,
there was outrage. The massacre sparked protests throughout the country, and the
British responded with more violence. Word eventually reached King George VI,
who launched an official investigation under the auspices of the Lucknow High
Court. The court's report documented the massacre for posterity and concluded
that the egregious violence of the British troops was unjustified.[47]

Thousands rallied around the jail where Khan was held, although his brother
ensured that they remained nonviolent. This prompted the British to move Khan
from the Frontier to Gujarat, where he found himself in the company of Muslim, Sikh, and Hindu political prisoners from throughout the region. "Never, in
any other prison, has it been my good fortune to spend such happy days in the
congenial company of learned religious and political leaders," he later wrote. "It
was of the greatest benefit to me."[48] Back on the Frontier, the British imposed a
lockdown on the province and set fire to the offices of the Khudai Khidmatgars
in Utmanzai. Members, recognizable by their red garments, were rounded up for

repeated beatings and imprisonment. Losing the Frontier meant the loss of India, the British believed, so the oppression there was greater than anywhere else on the subcontinent. British brutality, however, evoked the latent patriotism of Pashtuns yet to join Khan, and they defiantly donned red garments, too. In the face of growing oppression, the resistance grew in equal measure. "The British feared a nonviolent Pashtun more than a violent one," Khan observed.[49]

As he sat alone in his small, dark prison cell, Khan's colleagues met with representatives of the All-India Muslim League and asked for their help. At the very least, they could tell the world about the atrocities taking place on the Frontier. But the league supported an alliance with the British against the majority Hindus and sought a separate Muslim state (i.e., Pakistan). It would not support the Khudai Khidmatgars or denounce the British. Crushed by the betrayal, the Khudai Khidmatgars officially joined the Indian National Congress. In response, the Congress promised its support for the Muslim peoples on the Frontier.[50] The alliance shook the British. Eager to fix the situation, they offered to improve conditions if the Khidmatgars would withdraw. But Khan did not trust the British and refused their offer. The Congress soon sent news about the plight of the Frontier throughout the country and far overseas.

On March 5, 1931, the Gandhi-Irwin Pact released all political prisoners, except for Badshah Khan. The Khidmatgars immediately sent a delegation to Gandhi to call for his release. Heeding their cries, Gandhi arranged a meeting with Lord Irwin, the viceroy of India, to negotiate his release, after which Khan, despite his weakened state, immediately returned to work on the Frontier against the British. The villagers even started to see Khan as a saint, and all throughout India he was called "the Frontier Gandhi." Of course he still had enemies as well. Traveling to Utmanzai, he survived the first of two assassination attempts. Then on December 24, 1931, the British again arrested Khan and thousands of other Pashtuns. "In jail I had nothing to do except read the Qur'an," he later wrote. "I read about the Prophet Muhammad in Mecca, about his patience, his suffering, his dedication; I had read it all before, as a child, but now I read it in the light of what I was hearing all around me about Gandhi's struggle against the British."[51] The persecution seemed to only increase his resolve and devotion to his cause.

The British could not end the Khidmatgars' nonviolent resistance with persecution, negotiations, bribes, or propaganda, so they sought to goad them into violence. "The British had been able to deal with the violent [resistance] movement by taking violent measures," Khan wrote, "but they had not been able to suppress the nonviolent movement in spite of all their unspeakable cruelty." Violence, he asserted, created disunity, fear, and cowardice, and weakened the morale of the Pashtuns, but nonviolence made the people "fearless and brave and inspired them with a high sense of morality."[52]

The British tried to provoke the Pashtuns with humiliation and torture. In one tactic, they stripped the men naked and tied ropes with a slip-knot around their testicles. "When the men fainted from the pain," Khan wrote, "they would be thrown into a tub full of urine and excrement."[53] Other times men were doused with ice water in the fierce cold of winter and deprived of blankets. Another method was to whip Pashtuns and force them to turn the wheel of an oil press as slaves. But the Khudai Khidmatgars endured, and these provocations failed to drive them into violence.

Emaciated and ill from influenza, Khan was released in August of 1934. He and his brother were forbidden from entering the Frontier or even the neighboring province. They traveled instead and spoke to gatherings of impoverished Muslims from Bengal. Encouraged by their response, Badshah Khan traveled to villages in Bengal and addressed crowd after crowd. While he is often described as a Pashtun nationalist, Khan's work among the Muslims of Bengal testified to his commitment to all Muslims, and it made him all the more dangerous. His activities in Bengal also drew the ire of the British, and he was arrested yet again, less than four months after his last release. He would not return to the Frontier until 1937. In his absence the Khudai Khidmatgars won a majority of seats in the 1936 Provincial Assembly of the North-West Frontier Province.[54]

The Partition

When World War II began, many Indians advocated support for Britain in exchange for India's independence at the war's conclusion. Both Khan and Gandhi rejected the idea, as it compromised their commitment to nonviolence. The Congress initiated a massive campaign of civil disobedience known as the Quit India Movement or August Movement. On the Frontier, Khan consulted with elders about carrying it out. One strategy employed by the Pashtuns was sabotaging

British communications and transports by cutting telephone wires and removing railway ties, but Khan instructed the saboteurs to go to the police and tell them what they had done each time. "This would make [the saboteur] develop moral courage and this would be an inspiration to other workers," he wrote. "Also, no innocent people would come under suspicion and the police would have no excuse for hunting and harassment."[55] Arrests of the Congress leadership soon followed. On October 27, 1942, Khan was arrested and spent the rest of the war in prison.

After his release in 1945, Khan, seriously ill, resumed his work. The issue of the day was partition and whether a unified India or a separate Muslim state was best. The Muslim League, led by Muhammad Ali Jinnah, advocated partition and asked Muslims, "Are you going to give your vote to the mosque or to the temple?"[56] Khan, however, supported the idea of a united India. He believed that the Muslim Pashtuns would enjoy better rights in a large, decentralized, pluralist Indian state. However, when the British viceroy pushed the issue and held a referendum in 1947 to settle the matter, the Khidmatgars refused to participate. "The British," Khan wrote, "never wanted to see harmony and concord between the Hindus and the Muslims, and they were determined to divide the country."[57] He believed the British were trying to make their rule appear necessary, claiming that if Britain left India "the Indians would destroy each other in no time."[58] Freedom, however, was now inevitable. The only question was in what condition the British would leave the subcontinent when they left in defeat.

The British Parliament passed the Indian Independence Act in 1947, and the partition of India commenced, resulting in mass displacement and as many as one million deaths in Hindu-Muslim-Sikh communal violence. Khan pledged his allegiance to the new state of Pakistan but advocated an autonomous Pashtun state for his people to be truly free. The new leaders of Pakistan, in turn, arrested him for fomenting sedition in 1948 and imprisoned him for most of the next fifteen years, seeing him as a threat to the territorial integrity of the new state. The Khudai Khidmatgars were outlawed, its members were jailed—even killed—and their offices were burned to the ground. "Thousands of *Khudai Khidmatgars* lost their lives," Khan later wrote, and "they were not only imprisoned, but treated very badly and cruelties that no man can endure were inflicted upon them."[59]

Khan's sons were imprisoned, too, but survived to serve as leaders for the next generation. However, tragedy struck the family in May of 1958. Dr. Khan Sahib, who was serving as a minister in Pakistan's government despite his brother's objections, was assassinated by a disgruntled government employee. He was buried in the family village of Utmanzai.

Badshah Khan's fifteen years in Pakistan's prisons destroyed his health. On January 30, 1964, while gravely ill, he was finally released and left Pakistan for treatment in London. Upon invitation from King Zahir Shah, he went to recover in Afghanistan, where he remained for six years. In Kabul he wrote his autobiography in Pashto, later translated into English as *My Life and Struggle*, and he traveled the countryside speaking among the people, even to the most remote regions.

Regarded with hostility in Pakistan, Khan was a state guest in India in 1969 for the centennial of Gandhi's birth. During his visit, he was awarded the Nehru Award for International Understanding. Prior to his arrival, riots broke out and many Muslims were killed by a Hindu mob. The government tried to conceal the incident, until a Hindu leftist informed Khan and led him to a Muslim refugee camp.[60] Greatly troubled, Khan spoke out against communal violence between Hindus and Muslims and announced a three-day fast in protest, stating that selfish people had exploited religion for economic and political gain.[61] It was this sort of violence that had claimed the life of his dear friend Gandhi, who was shot by a Hindu extremist in 1948.

In December 1972 Khan returned home, where great crowds greeted him. Worn down by time, with his beard as white as the mountain snows that feed the Indus River, he continued his fight for peace, democracy, and a Pashtun homeland. He never wavered, even as he faced the disapproval of the regime and imprisonment throughout his remaining years, despite his advanced age. Pakistan's military regime even arrested him at the age of ninety-five when he protested against their undemocratic rule. He was a nonviolent soldier to the end.

After suffering a stroke in 1987, Badshah Khan died in a Peshawar hospital on January 20, 1988, while in a coma. The warring factions in Afghanistan, torn apart by the Soviet invasion, observed a ceasefire to honor his funeral, although two blasts still occurred and claimed the lives of mourners.[62] Altogether, tens-of-thousands accompanied his body through the Khyber Pass to his burial place in

Jalalabad. Meanwhile, the governments of India and Pakistan declared a period of official mourning.[63] Today his memory lives on among his people in the stories of his great struggles and among the Awami National Party led by his descendents, as well as humanitarian institutions such as the Badshah Khan Trust in Peshawar.

The Legacy of Badshah Khan

Considering the remarkable nature of his story, why is Badshah Khan not as widely known as other champions of nonviolence, such as Gandhi? There are several key reasons. The narrative of India's independence movement positioned Gandhi as the father of his nation. India is a country with a Hindu majority. Rather than crediting Badshah Khan as an equal beside Gandhi, perhaps uncomfortable with a champion who hails from the Muslim minority, India has treated Khan as the "Frontier Gandhi" or the "Second Gandhi." These are honorable designations, but they depict him as a secondary figure and a mere follower of Gandhi, rather than a man of his own personal, intellectual, and religious principles.

Meanwhile, in the Muslim state of Pakistan, Khan drew the ire of the government because he opposed the partition and advocated a homeland for the Pashtuns. As I have described, he was imprisoned and brutally treated in Pakistan for these reasons. Pakistanis in general have therefore excluded him from their national narrative. It is only among the Pashtuns themselves that he is revered.

The fact that he survived assassination attempts, unlike King or Gandhi, may have also limited the emergence of his narrative and legacy as well. Martyrdom, tragic though it may be, can transform an individual into an iconic symbol for a cause. Nevertheless, Badshah Khan's narrative is certainly a story worth telling, especially in light of the violence that plagues the modern world.

5

The Philosopher

The life of Badshah Khan is certainly worthy of emulation. But every social movement, nonviolent or otherwise, needs an intellectual to express the ideas behind it. Someone has to systematically present those views in a defensible manner. For every César Chávez, there must be a Martin Luther King Jr. In the case of Islamic nonviolence, that intellectual is likely Shaykh Jawdat Saeed, who has written numerous books, given countless lectures, and appeared on media outlets such as al-Jazeera Arabic satellite television. Now approaching eighty years of age, Saeed remains intellectually and physically active on his small farm in southern Syria and works from his home. On his official website, a surprising thing in itself, Saeed is shown sitting in his modest office with photographs of Gandhi, Martin Luther King Jr., and Abdul Ghaffar Khan beside him on his bookshelf. If there is a philosopher of Islamic nonviolence today, Jawdat Saeed is the one.

The Early Years

Saeed was born on February 9, 1931, in the small Circassian village of Bir Ajam, in the rich farmlands of the Golan Heights of Syria. His family was Sunni Muslim and adhered to the Hanafi school of law, which has long been common among the Circassians. Saeed's father, Muhammad, sent his son to study at a school in Quneitra, an Ottoman-era city that was later destroyed during the Arab-Israeli wars. Upon completing his studies, Saeed traveled to Cairo and attended the prestigious Islamic seminary there, al-Azhar University. Cairo was the center of the

Arab-Islamic renaissance (*al-nahda*) of the late nineteenth and early twentieth centuries, when scholars such as Jamal al-Din al-Afghani, Muhammad Abduh, and Rashid Rida achieved international renown. The city remained a cultural and intellectual hotbed of new religious and sociopolitical ideas. In 1952, the year of Gamal Abdel Nasser's anticolonial revolution, Saeed graduated from al-Azhar with a degree in Arabic studies and literature, as well as a diploma in education. It was the beginning of a long and accomplished intellectual life.

In 1950s Cairo Saeed was introduced to the work of Malik Bennabi, an Algerian scholar educated in Paris. Bennabi settled in Cairo in 1954, when the Algerian armed resistance against French colonial rule began, returning to Algeria in 1962 after independence. He produced over two dozen books, including *Les Conditions de la Renaissance* and *Le Problème des Idées dans le Monde Musulman,* until his death in 1973. "What Bennabi was saying was very different from what we used to hear from [Jamal al-Din] al-Afghani and Muhammad Abduh, and even [Sir Muhammad] Iqbal," Saeed recalled in a 1998 interview. "It was such a jolt to me when he refrained from blaming the enemies, the colonizer, the imperialist, the crusader, the Zionist, the freemason, and all the other foes."[1]

Bennabi's many writings tackled the subjects of culture, intellectual dynamism, and the means of development in Arab and Muslim society. He argued that modern Muslim backwardness must be understood in terms of ideas, not in terms of the acquisition of "objects" such as weapons and technologies, because social development should increasingly be understood through intellectual criteria.[2] "The morbid adoration in the Muslim world for physical force has hindered its appreciation of knowledge and the power of ideas," Bennabi argued, "that ideas are the real resource of the people."[3] He also criticized the Muslim tendency to resort to apologetics and to rely on past accomplishments of Islamic civilization rather than look to future goals and achievements. In addition to the ideas of Bennabi, Saeed also took great interest in the works of Sir Muhammad Iqbal.

Muhammad Iqbal was a Punjabi philosopher, Sufi mystic, and poet educated in England and Germany, who emphasized the need to spiritually and politically revitalize modern Islam, most notably in a book of collected lectures titled *The Reconstruction of Islamic Thought.*[4] Saeed credited Iqbal with awakening Muslims to the idea that even though "the Qur'an and Islam emerged before the age of science, it was the Qur'an which heralded the age of science" and that the Qur'an demonstrates "the importance of the facts of the real world and human experience." These insights from Iqbal led Saeed to embrace the idea that "the truth" is discernable by looking at the sort of human being that a doctrine, philosophy, or belief produces. He cites Iqbal's teaching that "Allah's *sharia* [i.e., law] is realized when justice is realized; whatever comes closer to justice is closer to Allah's sharia." This idea enabled Saeed to see beyond the restrictive parameters that were set in the past and reenvision Islam in the present. Muslims, according to Saeed, must be completely free to go beyond the "dogmatic mind." The "dogmatic mind," Saeed explains, "is the mind of a person who, when the objective circumstances call for a change in attitude, fails to make that change."[5]

The Sons of Adam

When he returned to his native Syria, Saeed completed mandatory military service and worked as a teacher in the historic capital of Damascus. Although details are lacking, Saeed maintained an association with the Muslim Brotherhood (Ikhwan al-Muslimun) during this time, probably stemming from his time in Egypt—the birthplace of the Islamist movement—and his ideas earned him the ire of Syrian government authorities. The prominent Tunisian Islamist leader, Rachid Ghannouchi, encountered Saeed during those years in Damascus, later describing him as a very distinguished personality and an "active volcano."[6] Saeed, however, grew estranged from the militant current of the Islamist movement at that time, as well as the turbulent political scene of the region. By the 1960s Saeed was issuing a forceful rebuke of the militant Egyptian ideologue Sayyid Qutb in the form of an Arabic treatise titled *Madhhab Ibn Adam al-Awal* (*The Doctrine of the First Son of Adam*). It was the first of his writings on Islamic nonviolence.

Saeed's treatise, first published in 1965, is an exposition of Islamic nonviolence rooted in the story in the Qur'an of Adam's two sons, Cain and Abel. This classic account (known in a prior form in the Bible) is related in the fifth chapter, which dates from the Medinan period after the hijra. Although it shares the core elements with the Genesis story in the Torah, the Qur'anic version contains some unique elements:

Recite to them the story of the sons of Adam in truth. Behold! They each presented a sacrifice (to God). It was accepted from one, but not from the other. The latter said, "Surely I will kill you." "Surely," said the former, "God accepts the sacrifice of those who are righteous. If you stretch out your hand against me to kill me, it is not for me to stretch my hand against you, for I do fear God, the Lord of the Worlds. For me, I intend to let you draw on yourself my sin as well as yours, for you will be among the companions of the fire, and that is the reward of those who do wrong." The selfish soul of the other led to the murder of his brother. He murdered him and became one of the lost ones.[7]

Abel's refusal to respond with retaliatory violence, as related in the preceding verses, is the principal Qur'anic paradigm of nonviolence. It should be noted again that the Qur'an is not an account of Muhammad's life story. Therefore, Badshah Khan's emphasis on the Meccan period of Muhammad's life is not at all in conflict with the fact that this passage is Medinan. In the Qur'an, Abel died as a righteous martyr rather than retaliating with violence and becoming a "selfish soul" who disobeyed God, as his brother Cain had done when he committed murder.

Another important story in the Qur'an relates an event that occurred prior to Abel's murder. This is the story of the creation of humanity and the formation of Adam out of dust and water mixed into clay. It states that when the angels in heaven heard that God was planning to appoint his newest creation, Adam, and his descendents as his viceroy over the earth, the angels protested to God, saying, "Will Thou place in the earth one who will make mischief and shed blood?"[8] The objection by the angels before God would prove to be prophetic, because as a result of the primordial murder committed by Cain, humanity would spring from the loins of a murderer, and subsequently all humans would "carry the virus of Adam's corrupt first son" who faced his problems with violence.[9] As such, "the doctrine represented by the attitude of Adam's first son toward the first dispute which took place at the onset of humanity will be a crest [to be overcome] for humanity on its long march."[10] In Saeed's view, human beings must follow God's guidance and progress forward to find new, constructive ways of solving their problems in an atmosphere that is "free from any threat of bloodshed, revenge or spirit of retaliation and aggression."[11] For "violence is not a disease afflicting only youth," Saeed writes. "The whole world suffers from this lethal disease."[12]

Saeed devotes great attention to the stories in the Qur'an about the prophets, such as Jesus and Moses. He notes that their mission to spread the call of God (dawa) and establish an Islamic way of life had two distinct stages. "Some were able to complete the two stages, such as Moses and Muhammad," writes Saeed, "while others did not go further than the first stage, such as Christ."[13] The first stage consists of calling people to God using proofs and righteous conduct, never imposing any beliefs upon society through coercion, and enduring the hostility and opposition of unbelievers with patience. When a society is undertaking the process of becoming a "true" Islamic society, Muslims cannot issue judgments, "especially in those matters related to the shedding of blood and personal rights."[14] It is only when a society finally becomes a truly Islamic one, accepting the laws and norms of God's religion (i.e., Islam), that the second stage begins and force to sustain the social order becomes necessary. This was the case in the city of Medina under the Prophet Muhammad (i.e., the Medinan period) and among the Israelites under Moses in the Sinai.

The second stage of the prophets' mission, following the first stage of propagation, does not abrogate peaceful and nonviolent methods of reform and resistance, even though an Islamic society has been established. Nonviolence remains the ethical ideal, but Saeed concedes that force may be used as a last resort if preceded by the approval or consensus of society. It is not acceptable for an individual to perpetrate violence on his own accord. People must be free to declare and propagate their faith in "the One God" and suffer for that cause alone (not for engaging in criminal behavior), as the prophets were persecuted for no other reason than their simple declaration of monotheism. This view contradicts the idea of revolutionary violence against a "*jahili* society" (i.e., infidel society) carried out by an Islamic "vanguard" as articulated by Sayyid Qutb. In fact, Saeed considers Qutb's ideology to be an inversion of the truth, which is that nonviolent propagation is the way to guide a deviant society, rather than by force, violence, or imposing laws on people. "*Jihad* and applying the laws in Islam are not the means of spreading Islam," Saeed writes. "Rather they are intended as tools to abolish oppression."[15] Achieving a true Islamic society, according to Saeed, can never be achieved by the use of force.[16]

Saeed contends that the manipulation of the concept of jihad "has probably caused more harm to Muslims than any other malpractice."[17] Indeed, due to this affliction, those who use jihad as a violent tool for coercion and shedding blood "must be quelled with any possible means," not only because they are terrorists, but because "they are also trying to distort and corrupt Islam."[18] The best form of jihad is courageously declaring the truth in the face of falsehood and tyranny, and accepting the repercussions for doing so with unwavering conviction. This was demonstrated by one of the first Muslims, Bilal, who was an Abyssinian companion of the Prophet and former slave who was tortured for his belief in the One God by his pagan master in Mecca.

The question of force inevitably raises the question of infidelity, or *kufr*, and the place of unbelievers within an Islamic society during the second stage. Saeed cites a well-known Medinan verse from the Qur'an: "Let there be no compulsion in religion; the Truth is henceforth clear from error."[19] In keeping with the principles of orthodox Sunni theology, Saeed reminds his readers that "belief that is the result of compulsion is not belief, nor is disbelief."[20] Based on this important Qur'anic principle, the disbelievers, namely those who oppose the call and deny the existence of the One God, cannot be harmed so long as they themselves are not violating the same imperative. For, as noted, an Islamic society can defend itself against destruction. However, Saeed argues:

> If we were to imagine or assume that Islam could never be accepted by others unless it was forced upon them, then we would be highly deceived and detached from the justice of Islam. It would be as if the human mind, created by God, could not be approached by logic.[21]

Unbelievers have the right to exist peacefully in an Islamic society, enjoying the same rights as Muslims to debate and express their views. As Saeed states, the "right of protecting people's thoughts and beliefs is to be applied to believers in the same way that it is to be applied to unbelievers," and they "have the same right as believers do in calling people to their ideas, in a peaceful way, disputing in a gracious way."[22] Saeed's assertion is a reference to the Qur'anic verse, "Call [others] to the path of your Lord with wisdom and beautiful preaching and debate with them in ways that are best."[23] Most Islamists—perhaps even Muslims in general—would object to the idea of letting atheists or polytheists call people to their "blasphemous" ideas. For some, the idea is unthinkable. "Not many Muslims at present tolerate granting to others the right to call to their ideas, in an equal degree as they (Muslims) believe they are privileged to have," writes Saeed. "The reason is that they do not have enough confidence in the ideas, or in the religion they hold."[24] Ultimately, by letting this free and peaceful discourse take place, Saeed believes that the Truth (quoting the Qur'an) will settle down as "the scum disappears like froth cast out; while that which is for the good of humanity remains on the earth."[25]

To support his position, Saeed relates the famous tale of the caliph Ali ibn Abu Talib (Imam Ali) in the seventh century. During the disputed reign of this son-in-law of the Prophet, two Muslim armies faced one another at the plain of Siffin in 657 on the banks of the Euphrates River. The Muslim community, still in its relative infancy, was terribly divided politically. Seeking to avoid any further Muslim bloodshed, Ali agreed to arbitration with his opponent, Muawiyya, in hopes of peacefully resolving the conflict. But a group of Ali's supporters disagreed with his decision, insisting that no such arbitration should take place and that the forces of Muawiyya were sinners who must be fought. Nevertheless, Ali went forward with the arbitration, which did not result favorably for him, and the dissenters rebelled against Ali, declaring him an apostate and proclaiming that the Qur'an alone had authority in such matters.

These rebels came to be known as *al-khawarij* ("the outsiders"), or Kharijites. They are often described as the first heretics and extremists in Islam. The Kharijites subsequently carried out acts of violence against the followers of Ali and Muawiyya, all the while proclaiming their devotion to the Qur'an and Islam. The Kharijites are further synonymous with the doctrine of *takfir*, the accusation of apostasy or unbelief against Muslims who do not meet their rigid standards of observance (thus forfeiting life and property). For Saeed the Kharijites epitomize the way that Muslims have deviated from the way of the prophets. "The Kharijites are people who were intent on establishing a society on the basis of compulsion," he writes, and their error, regrettably, has never left the Muslim community.[26] Saeed remarks, "Let the Kharijites be jubilant in their graves, seeing that the whole Muslim world has converted to their way; that the 'conditions for lawful jihad' of the other Muslims are no better than those of the Kharijites."[27]

Defending the Doctrine

Amid the pervasive violence in the modern Middle East, Saeed's concept of non-violence has been the target of criticism from many sides. One prominent criticism of nonviolence is the idea that it connotes being passive, weak, and impotent to do anything in the face of injustice. As Saeed states, "such people argue that the use of this approach should denote impotence and weakness, and that whoever adopts such a [nonviolent] approach is actually trying to disguise his own personal weakness by the promotion of such an approach."[28] This is a common critique against nonviolence in all cultures, including America's.

Saeed responds by asserting that "these claims only prove that those who adopt them have failed to understand the [nonviolent] approach, and that the approach, in itself, is a mystery to them," because nonviolent resistance is "the actual field of struggle [i.e., jihad] and positive action."[29] Nonviolence, additionally, is "more reassuring to the conscience" and strategically superior, because "those who may be imprisoned for adopting this approach are never worried that the authorities will discover the other side to their actions, because their actions have neither other sides nor secrets." Furthermore, he notes, those factions of society and world powers that oppose Islam under the pretext of opposing "terrorism" will "no longer be able to hide behind the screen of such accusations," and they will be "absolutely revealed to all people."[30] In other words, the justification for hostilities that is employed by the unbelievers will cease to exist, leaving their enmity and aggression unmasked for all to see. Saeed states, "If our aspiration is to deliver the Word of God, why do we help the enemies of our religion by provoking certain actions which give them the chance to carry out their plans?"[31]

In 1972 Saeed published a new treatise titled *Hatta Yughayyiru Ma Bi-Anfusihim* (*Until They Change What Is in Themselves*), a title derived from a well-known verse in the Qur'an. The foreword to the book was written by the aforementioned scholar Malik Bennabi during a time when he resided in Tripoli,

Lebanon. "Brother Jawdat Saeed knows, as a Muslim well versed in Islamic culture," Bennabi wrote, "that change, throughout history, yields to the law of the self (*al-nafs*)."[32] Saeed asserts that scholars and activists who have contemplated social issues, ills, and injustices, offering creative understandings and solutions, lack the underlying principle that lies at the heart of the matter, which is "the self." The Qur'an, Saeed argues, teaches humanity that all of their predicaments are the product of the self, so the problem "is not the injustice (*al-zulum*) that befalls humanity from the outside, but what descends upon humanity from itself (*binafsihu*)."[33]

While rooted in the Qur'an, this argument is certainly aligned with Bennabi's views, specifically his criticism of the Muslim world for its preoccupation with blaming its ills on the Other—the colonizer, the Zionist, and so forth. Saeed contends that people who fail to truly understand the creed (*aqida*) of Islam have tried to cure society of its ills by imposing laws or using force to change its conditions, even by waging war on an Other. He also criticizes those resigned to fatalistically accepting the problems of the world, awaiting the messianic Mahdi or the End Times to set things right. In a clearly activist stance, Saeed asserts that change must begin within the individual and proceed forth like the cells of a larger organism before God will change the conditions of a community or society as a whole. This argument directly undermines the narrative of violence, which invites audiences to see the harm or destruction of an outside Other as the path to change.

The 1973 Arab-Israeli War reclaimed a portion of the Golan Heights from Israeli occupation, and Saeed returned to Bir Ajam (which had been evacuated since the Six-Day War in 1967). He worked there as a farmer and wrote works of Islamic thought and philosophy, engaging the ideas of scholars such as Algerian intellectual Mohammed Arkoun and French Nietzschean Michel Foucault. Arkoun, a professor at the Sorbonne, incorporated the social scientific tradition of French poststructuralism into the field of Islamic studies, identifying theoretical tensions and formulating important questions about how to rethink Islam in the contemporary world. "Arkoun has the distinction of having freed himself of the tendency, so prevalent in the Muslim world," Saeed remarks, "to take things to be either faultless or worthless."[34]

Arkoun became well known among scholars for his concept of the "un-thought" or "unthinkable" in Islamic thought, a concept that Saeed would incorporate into his own work. Saeed asks, "It is at this moment unthinkable that one refrains from killing if commanded to kill; how long will it take us to get out of our darkness?" He goes on to recall the stories of the Prophet's companions Bilal, Amar, Sumayya, and Yasir, who suffered greatly for their faith. These early Muslims "succeeded in getting out of obeying the oppressor and doing what he dictated; they simply held their hand back, and that is the real kernel of belief in the One God: to get out of being enslaved to the *taghoot* [i.e., false idols, including rulers]." He concludes, "That is why I say: instead of seeing the young Islamists being imprisoned or put to death or tortured for attempting to kill someone, I would prefer that they are tortured, put to death, or imprisoned because they have refused to kill." Nonviolence must be sprung from the prison of the "unthinkable" in Islamic thought, making people unafraid to challenge the violent militancy of Islamic extremists and appreciate the ideas of thinkers such as Gandhi and King. After all, for a Muslim to simply follow a ruler or cleric who commands Muslims to fight and kill is a form of polytheism, because "belief in the One God does not allow you to obey anyone when their command is contrary to God's command." [35]

In his 1988 book *Iqra wa Rabuk al-Akram* (*Read! And Your Lord Is Most Gracious*), Saeed argued that scientific knowledge is essential to human progress and its neglect in the modern Muslim world is contrary to the Qur'anic message with its commands to "read!" and acquire knowledge throughout the earth. There is an element of Arkoun in such assertions. However, Saeed couches his message in scriptural hermeneutics, which is alien to Arkoun, who would actually rebuke such an approach. Saeed is, after all, the product of an Islamic seminary, and his project is fundamentally religious in nature, even Islamist (broadly construed). For example, he asserts in the introduction, "For [read] was the first word that was revealed of the last revelation [i.e., the Qur'an], before any other word of the creed, belief, or practice [of Islam]." [36] Saeed's reading of the Qur'an puts human experience and the natural world at the forefront of knowledge. He devotes much of the third section of his book to the Qur'an's call in the twenty-ninth chapter, "Travel throughout the earth and examine how creation began." [37] The era of prophethood came to a close with Muhammad. Humanity must therefore move forward using as a guide its God-given rational intellect and the knowledge it acquires. To renounce science and knowledge out of devotion to revelation is contrary to the message of the Qur'an itself, according to Saeed. This pursuit of knowledge, shared among Muslims and non-Muslims, is an important avenue to peace around the world.

Making Waves

It is noteworthy that Jawdat Saeed's ideas have received attention in Islamist circles, and some of his views are evident in the writings of moderate Islamists such as the late Umar al-Tilmisani, the third supreme guide of the Muslim Brotherhood in Egypt. Tilmisani, who could possibly have warranted a chapter in this book himself, assumed leadership in the wake of the disastrous impact that violence had on Egyptian Islamist circles. He rejected violence and terrorism, and encouraged civil and legal channels for protest against the Egyptian regime.[38] The Muslim Brotherhood has since emphasized the importance of dawa, the call to Islam—and not revolutionary violence to overthrow the government—as the means to create an Islamic society. In fact, the official website of Egypt's Muslim Brotherhood has featured an article (originally from another website) discussing Jawdat Saeed's views on Islam and nonviolence.[39] It would be a mistake and an overstatement to be too encouraged by this, though, and think that Saeed's ideas have been fully adopted by moderate Islamists like Egypt's powerful Muslim Brotherhood. That is not the case. Rather, it simply indicates the significance of Saeed's views as part of an important and ongoing discourse in the Muslim world that has not been (or cannot be) simply dismissed.

6

The Martyr

History reveals that martyrdom can transform an individual into a powerful iconic symbol for a cause that far transcends the impact or ability of an individual in his or her lifetime. The execution of Mahmoud Muhammad Taha of Sudan in 1985 has contributed greatly (albeit tragically) to his international renown as a champion of Islamic nonviolence. However, interest in his life and teachings has remained sporadic at best. Following the terrorist attacks in the United States of September 11, 2001, several Western media outlets, such as *The New Yorker*, published stories that portrayed Taha as the elusive and little-known "Muslim Gandhi" that the world so desperately needs. Beyond these instances, though, Taha's legacy has been left largely to the students and followers who survived him among the Ikhwan al-Jumhuriyyun (Republican Brotherhood), most notably the Sudanese-American legal scholar Abdullahi Ahmed an-Naim. The task has proved to be a challenging one, because preserving Taha's legacy has also meant defending his teachings against persistent charges of heresy.

The Early Years

Sudan is a vast and desolate place, dependent on the lifeblood of the Nile. Once home to the great civilization of the Nubians and its mysterious monuments of stone, today the people of Sudan live in dusty modern cities and humble villages. Mahmoud Muhammad Taha was born in Rufa'a, a village near the confluence of the Blue Nile and White Nile, around 1910. Orphaned as a small child, Taha was raised by his aunt as a member of the Rikabiyya clan, who trace their ancestry to

Husayn ibn Ali (Imam Husayn), the beloved grandson of the Prophet Muhammad. Sufi saints and holy men were a fixture of the pastoral clan's history. It was
a world where *jinn*, or spirits, afflicted human life, and those forces had to be
dealt with. Yet as a child of colonial Sudan, Taha also grew up to attend a British-
run university, Gordon Memorial College (now the University of Khartoum), in
the capital city of Khartoum, where he graduated with a degree in engineering
in 1936.[1] This was a transformative period in the history of Sudan and a break
from the past. After completing his studies, Taha worked as a civil engineer for
the British-run Sudan Railways, but he resigned shortly thereafter. He was a sup-
porter of Sudan's independence movement struggling for freedom from British
rule, but Taha could not ethically struggle for freedom against the British so long
as he took his wages from them. At the same time, the charismatic Taha could
not shoulder the burden of his struggle alone. In October 1945, Taha founded the
Republican Party (al-Hizb al-Jumhuri), an Islamic dawa association committed
to a fully independent Sudanese republic. The British promptly imprisoned him
for his efforts.[2]

That same year, the Republicans, better known as the Jumhuris, produced
a pamphlet that expressed their core positions. Titled *al-Sifr al-Awal* (*The First
Pamphlet*), it advocated Sudanese independence, democracy, and a republican
system of governance.[3] The small group distributed the pamphlet to the public
and spoke at mosques, clubs, cafés, and street corners.[4] Later the Jumhuris organized a public protest in Rufa'a against the arrest of a Sudanese woman who had
violated a newly implemented British law.

Away in prison, Taha took the opportunity to devote himself to prayer, fasting, and *dhikr*, the mystical devotions to God common among Sufis. He was
preparing himself for the challenges that lay ahead. Released in 1948, Taha chose
to enter into a period of ascetic seclusion, prayer, and fasting. He left his home
to live in a small mud hut in the courtyard of his in-laws in Rufa'a.[5] It was the
beginning of a new, radical stage in his remarkable life that would help shape the
future of Sudan.

The educated engineer and political activist who had strangely left behind
the world of politics and business quickly attracted the attention of the villagers and the serious concern of his family. The Rikabiyya clan was no stranger to

khalwas (mystical retreats) and the otherworldly lives of Sufi mystics, but Taha's behavior seemed extreme even to them.

Yet this behavior was hardly unprecedented among the great scholars and teachers of Islamic history. The great Sunni theologian, scholar, and mystic Abu Hamid al-Ghazali abandoned his prestigious post at a leading madrassa in Baghdad in the late eleventh century in order to devote himself to mystical contemplation of God, at one point undertaking a retreat in Jerusalem beside the sacred Dome of the Rock and al-Aqsa Mosque. That was long ago, though, and this was the modern world of the twentieth century. A family man, an engineer educated in a secular British university, was hardly a likely candidate for such eccentric religious pursuits. And unlike al-Ghazali, Taha had no connection to the corpus of religious knowledge overseen by the *ulama* (religious scholars), nor did he follow the traditional stages of the mystical path among the Sufis.[6] Taha's wife, Amna Lutfi, was even urged to divorce him, and some of the villagers suspected him of going insane.[7]

Spiritual Rebirth

The pernicious rumors of the village did not dissuade Taha from his spiritual quest. He spoke to very few people, ate only simple meals brought to him by his wife, and left his mud hut only to bathe in the nearby Nile. One contemporary observer described Taha as having long, wild hair and bloodshot eyes at the time.[8] His mission to uncover the "pure Islam" of the Prophet Muhammad lasted for some three years, and he emerged from his solitude in 1951 at around the age of forty. It was the same age as the Prophet Muhammad when he began his mission in Mecca following his spiritual retreat on Mount Hira.

Taha proclaimed that he had found the true meaning of the Qur'an. He described this knowledge, which he promised to teach to all who would listen, as the "second message of Islam." In response to his new mission, al-Hizb al-Jumhuri was realigned to serve as a more distinctly religious organization, and members who were inclined to secular politics left the group for other parties.[9] Taha, also known as Ustadh Mahmoud ("Teacher Mahmoud"), assumed a role akin to that of a Sufi *shaykh* or *pir* (master) in the movement, which increasingly resembled a *tariqa* (Sufi fraternity or association). Like those of many mystical associations in the Muslim world, some of the group's practices, based on Taha's teachings, drew sharp criticism from more "orthodox" Muslims and organizations. Among the most controversial was Taha's concept of "prayer by communion" (*salat al-sila*), as distinguished from traditional Muslim ritual prayer performed five times daily, which Taha called the "prayer of gestures" (*salat al-harakat*) or the "prayer of ascension" (*salat al-mir'aj*).[10] The "prayer by communion," in contrast, is offered at any and all times and consists of internal or mystical contemplation of God. Both forms of prayer had a place in Taha's vision of Islam, but it was the prayer of communion that held greater importance for him and his followers.

In 1955, three years after Gamal Abdel Nasser's "Free Officer" revolution ended British colonial rule in Egypt, neighboring Sudan was on the verge of its own independence. There was widespread debate about the future of the country and what system of government it should adopt. Taha chose to enter the national debate with the publication of a set of recommendations for the Sudanese constitution. He advocated the creation of a presidential, federal, democratic, and socialist republic, and he opposed the application of laws derived from Islamic sharia. Not only did existing Sudanese conceptions of sharia conflict with Taha's new understanding of "true Islam," but he believed that the application of sharia would foment animosity among Sudan's non-Muslims, especially in the culturally distinct South (now South Sudan).[11] The debates and political infighting ended abruptly, however, when a bloodless military coup on November 17, 1958, put Maj. Gen. Ibrahim Abbud in power and all political parties were dissolved.[12]

After the coup the Jumhuris remained on the margins of Sudan's political scene. The political landscape was dominated by the military and not the members of the dissolved political parties. Nevertheless, Taha sent a letter to Abbud, along with a copy of his book *Usus Dustur al-Sudan* (*Foundations for the Constitution of Sudan*). He encouraged the regime to consider applying the proposals espoused by the Jumhuris for a democratic, socialist federal government, but he was ignored. For the first two years of Abbud's military rule, Taha presented his teachings through constant public lectures, especially in the bustling northern cities of Khartoum and Omdurman, until the "orthodox" religious conservatives had him banned and the Jumhuris were forced to meet in private homes and were denied access to the state-controlled media.[13]

On July 17, 1963, Taha was interviewed by American scholar John Voll, currently a professor of Islamic studies at Georgetown University. Taha was asked to explain his understanding of Sufism (tasawwuf). He explained that "a Sufi is a man who tries to imitate the Prophet's way of life, namely, who tries to be true to himself, to his fellow men and to God, inasmuch as the Prophet was such."[14] Taha further explained that a true Islamic society is based on the "universality" that comes from peaceful self-realization, a process achieved through tasawwuf. This meant acquiring a correct outlook (or consciousness) toward the universe based on monotheism (*tawhid*) and a completely deterministic scheme based on God's absolute unity. As Taha explained:

> Every Sufi tries, through his spiritual development, to work his way up the ladder of consciousness, from limitation to abundance, from Man's opportunity, to God's proximity. At a certain stage along that ladder, discord gives place to harmony and the inner conflicts cool down. The individual enjoys eternal bliss. . . . Unity with God means sharing with Him his attributes of perfection. Individualism is one of these attributes. The successful Muslim must enjoy absolute individual freedom. Here Islam ceases to be a religion. It becomes a way of life. It gives to every individual his moral code.[15]

In Taha's view, the ideal form of government to enable the spiritual development of the individual to take place is a democracy, because liberty is a prerequisite for such development. Although Taha did not describe his political system as an "Islamic state," he refrained only because of the politicization of the concept by ignorant and ill-equipped political groups. He noted that "an Islamic state built on ignorance of the pure facts of Islam can be more detrimental to progress than a secular state of average ability."[16]

The October Revolution of 1964 peacefully brought an end to the Abbud regime and established a multiparty democracy in Sudan for a time.[17] However, the ideological chasm that existed between the political Left and Right drove the country back down the path of division, turmoil, and a looming constitutional crisis. The Sudanese branch of the Muslim Brotherhood, called the Islamic Charter Front, sought an amendment in the constitution to outlaw "atheistic" groups, which meant the influential Communist Party.[18] The Islamic Charter Front was led at the time by Hasan al-Turabi, a well-known Sudanese Islamist scholar educated in Khartoum, London, and Paris. Although Taha was a vocal critic of Marxist thought, he opposed al-Turabi's efforts on the grounds that they violated freedom of speech and association, and could even strengthen communism in the end.[19]

The Second Message

In 1967 Taha published his clearest articulation of the "true Islam"— the renewed Islam that he taught to his followers for humanity in the twentieth-century. In the book *al-Risala al-Thaniyya min al-Islam* (*The Second Message of Islam*), Taha discussed his views on the meaning of the Qur'an and addressed the subjects of individual freedom, the rights of women, and nonviolence. He emphasized a vital distinction between the Meccan and Medinan periods of the Prophet Muhammad's mission in Arabia, when lawless tribalism ruled the day. In Mecca, at the onset of his mission, the revelations of the Qur'an prohibited Muslims from fighting and instead counseled patience, perseverance, and righteousness in the face of adversity. During this period, Muhammad preached his message peacefully and did not impose or employ any means of coercion on the people. For Taha the Islam of the Meccan period was the definitive expression of the religion, the true and universal Islam. "Their lives [i.e., those of the early Muslims] were the supreme expression of their religion," Taha explained, "and consisted of sincere worship, kindness, and peaceful coexistence with all other people."[20] However, the people of Mecca had harshly opposed the monotheistic message of the Prophet, and they persecuted his community in order to eliminate it. Taha believed that these events postponed the establishment of "true Islam," as humanity proved unprepared for it, and a temporary form of Islam had been imposed until humanity could progress to a stage where it could implement the true, universal Islam. "Many aspects of the present Islamic sharia are not the original principles or objectives of Islam," Taha stated. "They merely reflect a descent in accordance with the circumstances of the time and the limitations of human ability."[21]

This temporary Medinan Islam, instituted through the Qur'anic revelations in the city of Medina between 622 and 632, utilized coercion and force in response to Meccan aggression against the Muslims. This was what Taha described as the "First Message" of Islam. "Religion," he wrote, was "lowered from its peak down to the level of human needs and capabilities, in the form of sharia." A harsh system of law and conduct, including the jihad of the sword, were imposed during the Medinan period to safeguard the community and preserve the social order against those who wished to abuse their freedom and deprive it from others. "Since at that time there was no law except the sword, the sword was used to that effect," explained Taha. "The sword was used to curtail the abuse of freedom."[22] The women in Medina also needed to observe certain restrictions and inequalities in response to those same circumstances. Ultimately, however, Taha believed that the Muslims of the late twentieth century, as well as humanity in general, had finally reached a level of consciousness where they could accept the "Second Message," meaning the "true Islam" of Mecca, and the temporary Islam that began in Medina—the Islam of warfare and ancient penal codes—could be abrogated. Taha stated that "since humanity has evolved over fourteen centuries, towards maturity, becoming, through the grace of God, materially and intellectually capable of implementing both socialism and democracy, Islam must be propagated in these terms."[23] The Jumhuris, therefore, emphasized the teachings of the Meccan revelations above all else in support of their social and political platform.

In the wake of the book's publication, Taha and the Jumhuris were accused of *ridda*, or apostasy from Islam. This was a most serious accusation as, according to the dominant view in Islamic jurisprudence, the punishment for ridda (pending repentance) is death. In November 1968 the Khartoum High Sharia Court heard allegations raised by two faculty members of the Islamic University of Omdurman who accused Taha of ridda and demanded the dissolution of al-Hizb al-Jumhuri, a ban on his publications, and the nullification of his marriage.[24] He was found guilty. Although the verdict had no formal consequences, the case did pose problems for the Jumhuris, and it cast the dangerous stigma of "heresy" over the movement. This controversial event was quickly overshadowed by growing political turmoil in Sudan, culminating in a military coup in May 1969 by the so-called Free Officers (modeled after Nasser's 1952 revolution in Egypt). The coup brought Col. Jafar Numayri into power, and all political parties, including the Jumhuris and the Islamic Charter Front, were once again outlawed.

In 1970 Taha officially changed the name of his organization to the Republican Brotherhood (Ikhwan al-Jumhuriyyun), replacing *hizb* or "political party" with *ikhwan* or brotherhood as Sufi orders are often known, in order to reflect the spiritual orientation of the movement, and he continued his public lectures despite "orthodox" and Islamist opposition. Taha's personality and character proved to be as vital to the survival of the movement as his teachings, and detractors often accused the Jumhuris of treating Taha as a new prophet. Those who knew Taha still recall his admirable self-control, patience, honesty, and simple way of life. "His honesty, his intellectual vigor, his serenity, his charisma—those are the things that we can observe, and from them I understood that this is someone who had a transformative religious experience," one of his followers later recalled.[25] Taha used to receive visitors at his home in Omdurman at all hours, teaching, listening, and answering questions.

Taha's public activities were eventually banned in 1973, but the Republican Brotherhood actually experienced its greatest growth in the 1970s and early 1980s, especially among women and literate young urbanites.[26] "Republican Sisters" participated fully in the group's activities and often served as leaders of activist groups at Sudanese universities, proselytizing in public parks and on street corners wearing their trademark simple white clothing.[27] The Jumhuris were particularly well known for their egalitarian reforms of the institution of marriage. Jumhuri husbands extended the unilateral right to divorce to their wives in marriage contracts, a rarity in Sudanese culture. The Jumhuris also dispensed with the custom of extravagant marriage ceremonies and exorbitant dowries that placed considerable burdens on families and discouraged young couples from getting married.[28]

Meanwhile, the political winds of the time moved Numayri's military regime toward the extreme Right. The regime reconciled with the Islamic Charter Front in 1976 and installed the Islamist ideologue al-Turabi as the nation's attorney general. The shift in the Numayri regime's ideological allegiances created the conditions for Taha's opponents to move against him once again. The "orthodox" had already obtained two fatwas (legal pronouncements) from Egypt's al-Azhar University in 1972 and Saudi Arabia's Muslim World League in 1975 branding Taha an apostate. Following the reconciliation between the Islamists and Numayri's regime, an organization of Sudanese ulama further submitted a memorandum to the People's Assembly that accused Taha of distorting Islam and conspiring with foreign powers against the Sudanese state.[29] The "orthodox" interest in Taha and the Jumhuris, however, had little to do with correct beliefs and more with silencing political dissent against the regime, especially among Sudan's youth. Taha, after all, adamantly opposed the Islamists' destructive political ambitions for his homeland.

To the Gallows

By the 1980s Numayri had exhausted one political model after another, including Marxism and Arab nationalism, in order to justify his authoritarian rule, but his regime was continuing to weaken, and he apparently felt threatened by the popularity of Attorney General al-Turabi.[30] Numayri thus turned to Islamism as a last resort and declared that he would impose sharia across Sudan, including the controversial *hudud* corporal punishments for crimes such as theft or adultery.[31] As a vocal opponent of Numayri's new Islamist ambitions, Taha and dozens of his followers, including the young Abdullahi an-Naim, were arrested without charge and imprisoned for months. By the time the Jumhuris were released in December 1984, numerous factions in Sudanese society had grown intent on aligning themselves against Taha and finishing what others had started in 1968.[32]

Shortly after his release, Taha wrote a controversial new pamphlet titled *Either This or the Flood*, in which he argued that Numayri's sharia plans "have distorted Islam in the eyes of intelligent members of our people and in the eyes of the world, and degraded the reputation of our country."[33] The pamphlet called for the repeal of the 1983 Penal Code (introducing hudud punishments), an immediate end to the civil war against the southern Sudanese, and advised greater study of the sunna (i.e., the way of the Prophet, or "true Islam"), stating that "our times call for sunna, not sharia."[34] When the Jumhuris, including female members, began to distribute the pamphlet on the street corners, the local police dealt with them leniently, although some arrests were made.[35] The regime, however, had other plans in mind and charged the leadership of the Jumhuris with the crime of sedition against the state.

On January 5, 1985, Taha was arrested and two days later brought to trial with four of his followers. Numayri, supported by al-Turabi and the Islamists, ordered that the penal code be amended in order to allow the court to pursue the punishment for the crime of apostasy (ridda).³⁶ A young judge, Hassan Ibrahim al-Mahalawy, with less than three years judicial experience, was appointed to preside over the proceedings.³⁷ At court Taha made a defiant statement, declaring, "I am not willing to cooperate with any court that has betrayed the independence of the judiciary and allowed itself to be used as a tool for humiliating the people, insulting free thought, and persecuting political opponents."³⁸ Nevertheless, on January 8, after a two-hour session the previous day, the judge issued his ruling. Rebuking Taha's teachings, al-Mahalawy strangely criticized the mystical knowledge that Taha had given to the common people declared him guilty on all charges, and sentenced him to death. Numayri moved to have Taha brought to the gallows as soon as possible.³⁹ Seeing this, the four Jumhuris on trial with Taha repented on state television and radio and denounced their "apostate" teacher. Their lives were spared by presidential pardon.

On the morning of January 18, 1985, Taha was brought before a large crowd in the Justice Square of Khartoum North Prison with his hands tied behind his back.⁴⁰ Among the onlookers was American journalist Judith Miller. She later recalled, "I managed to catch only a glimpse of Taha's face before the executioner placed an oatmeal-colored sack over his head and body, but I shall never forget his expression: His eyes were defiant; his mouth firm; he showed no hint of fear."⁴¹ As the Sudanese champion of nonviolence was hanged in a violent spectacle orchestrated by an inept and faltering regime, the crowd shouted victoriously, "God is great!" Afterward, Taha's body was whisked away by helicopter and discarded in the desert. Its location is still unknown.

Three months after the execution of Mahmoud Muhammad Taha, Numayri was overthrown in a coup that restored democratic rule in Sudan. As scholar Mohamed A. Mahmoud has noted, "The abhorrence and revulsion [to Taha's execution] felt by the majority of the Sudanese was undoubtedly an important catalyst that contributed to the regime's overthrow only eleven weeks after his execution."⁴² The coup was followed in February 1986 by a legal challenge as well. Taha's daughter Asma and one of his followers, Abdel-Latif Umar Hasab Allah, filed a constitutional lawsuit with the Supreme Court of Sudan. The new attorney general declared before the court on April 17, 1985, that the trial and execution of Mahmoud Taha by the regime of Jafar Numayri had been illegal and rife with constitutional and procedural violations.⁴³ When asked about Taha's death during an interview in 2000, Numayri claimed that he did not want to kill Taha, but that Attorney General al-Turabi had told him that Taha and the Jumhuris were siding with the Left against him to bring down his rule. He went on to say:

> I decided to postpone my decision for two days, and on the third day I went to Taha, dressed in civilian clothes. I told him, "Your death would sadden me. Just back down on your decision." But he spoke to me in a way that at the time I felt was blustering but now I see it was honorable, considering the situation. He told me, "*You* back down on *your* decision. As for me, I know that I'm going to be killed. If I'm not killed in court, the [Islamic Charter Front of Hasan al-Turabi] will kill me in secret. So leave and let me be. I know that I am going to die."⁴⁴

The Legacy of a Martyr

As it is often the case with martyrdom, the death of Mahmoud Taha did not mean the end of his ideas. On the contrary, one of his most gifted followers, the afore-mentioned Abdullahi Ahmed an-Naim, left to study in the United States where he published an English translation of Taha's seminal treatise, *al-Risala al-Thaniyya min al-Islam*. "One cannot exaggerate the importance of his humane and liberating understanding of Islam," an-Naim wrote in the book's 1987 introduction, "as an alternative to the cruel and oppressive interpretation underlying recent events in Iran, Pakistan, and Sudan, and the equally negative traditionalist view prevailing in Saudi Arabia and other parts of the Muslim world."⁴⁵ Since its initial publication, an-Naim has transformed Taha's mysticism into a rigorous intellectual project, publishing extensively on the "evolutionary principle of Ustadh Mahmoud" in works such as *Toward an Islamic Reformation: Civil Liberties, Human Rights, and International Law* and traveling the Muslim world speaking to crowds about an Islam that is free from violence, inequality, and compulsion.⁴⁶

This is the legacy of the martyr—a word whose Greek root means "witness." Taha's death was the clearest affirmation of his convictions and his commitment to Islamic nonviolence. The Jumhuris never waged a war and never carried out a campaign of terrorism against the state, either before or after the death of their leader. Yet the Numayri regime fell in a matter of weeks in the wake of Taha's execution. Even those Sudanese Muslims who were not Jumhuris felt the injustice and moral shame evident in the military power structure's treatment of the charismatic old man from Rufa'a. The Numayri regime's commitment to the narrative of violence sealed its own fate, as others have since. Even today one cannot speak the dictator Numayri's name without recalling the memory of Mahmoud Muhammad Taha, the heretic martyr of Sudan.

7

The Cleric

One of the most important differences between the Sunni and Shi'ite branches of Islam is the existence of a powerful clerical hierarchy among the Shi'ites. Sunni Muslims recognize learned scholars (ulama) and jurists as authorities for the community but lack anything comparable to the hierarchy of *mujtahids*, *hojjahs*, and ayatollahs in Shi'ite Islam, specifically its largest sect known as the Twelvers. ("Twelver" refers to the sect's recognition of twelve specific successors to Muhammad, the Holy Imams.) The highest rank attainable among the clerics of this centuries-old patriarchal hierarchy is grand ayatollah, who inherently becomes a *marja al-taqlid* ("source of emulation"). The success and validity of any Islamic concept in Shi'ite Islam, therefore, arguably requires the acceptance and endorsement of one of these elite, high-ranking clerics to prosper. Fortunately, nonviolence has already found one such proponent in the late Grand Ayatollah Muhammad ibn Mahdi al-Shirazi, the revered marja al-taqlid for millions of Shi'ite Muslims around the world.

The Early Years

Muhammad ibn Mahdi Hussaini al-Shirazi was born in 1928 into a prestigious Persian family of sayyids (descendants of the Prophet) and scholars in the Shi'ite holy city of Najaf, Iraq. Najaf is one of the foremost centers of Shi'ite learning and a site of religious pilgrimage, being the home of the sacred golden shrine of Ali ibn Abu Talib, revered as the first imam of Shi'ite Islam. The al-Shirazi clan, whose family name indicates its ancestral connection to the ancient Persian city of Shiraz, has long been a fixture of Shi'ite political activism throughout the Middle East. Two of the most notable al-Shirazi kinsmen were Grand Ayatollah Mirza Hassan al-Shirazi, leader of the constitutional and anti-colonial Tobacco Movement in nineteenth-century Iran, and Grand Ayatollah Muhammad Taqi al-Shirazi, leader of the 1920 revolt in Iraq against the British.[1]

As a boy, Muhammad ibn Mahdi al-Shirazi migrated with his family from Najaf to the holy city of Karbala, Iraq, where his younger brother Sadiq, later his successor, was born. Karbala is the second holiest city in Twelver Shi'ism, sometimes rivaling Mecca in the Wahhabite-Sunni country of Saudi Arabia. It was at Karbala in 680 that Imam Husayn ibn Ali, beloved grandson of the Prophet Muhammad and the third imam of Shi'ite Islam, sacrificed his life as a martyr for Islam against the tyranny and injustice of the Umayyad dynasty of caliphs. In reference to this sacred event, al-Shirazi claimed that "Gandhi, one of the activists in the liberation of India, used to say: 'I learnt from Imam Husayn how to attain victory while being oppressed.'"[2] The Battle of Karbala, as it is known, has since been immortalized among Shi'ite Muslims as the archetypal struggle between the forces of good and evil, the axis around which the universe spins. Passion plays and acts of self-mortification annually commemorate the tragic event on the holy day of Ashura.

The arrival of the al-Shirazi family to the holy city in 1937 solidified a deep spiritual connection with Karbala that superseded all other ties to the modern nation-states taking shape in the region. Muhammad al-Shirazi, throughout his life, never held Iraqi citizenship and vocally opposed nationalist identities on religious grounds, calling Karbala his homeland.[3] Such an assertion had deep spiritual resonance. Indeed, according to Shi'ite tradition, the very soil of Karbala is sacred and carries redemptive power, so much so that believers unable to be buried in the vicinity of the holy city still request to be buried with a small quantity of its soil.

Muhammad al-Shirazi's education in Karbala was completed under the tutelage of the esteemed scholars and clerics of his family, including his father, Grand Ayatollah Mahdi al-Shirazi. Karbala was also home to a prestigious *hawza*, or Islamic seminary, with a faculty that included many esteemed scholars. The young al-Shirazi reportedly excelled in his studies too, so much so that he achieved the clerical rank of mujtahid before the age of twenty, meaning he was competent to make independent juridical decisions. In February 1961 he published a collection of juridical edicts (*risala amaliyya*), a necessary step to becoming a marja al-taqlid, and at age thirty-three he became one.[4] Having achieved this esteemed clerical status, al-Shirazi was thereafter recognized as so learned in Islam that he was accepted as an authority for other Shi'ite Muslims to follow in their daily religious practice.[5]

The Message Begins

At the age of twenty-five, al-Shirazi commenced writing a monumental work on fiqh (Islamic jurisprudence) that grew to 150 volumes before his death and examined subjects such as the environment, economics, politics, freedom, systems of government, and nonviolence in Islam.[6] His systematic examination of nonviolence, found in volume 102 of the fiqh series, was later translated and reproduced by his supporters in a separate work titled *War, Peace, and Nonviolence: An Islamic Perspective*. Al-Shirazi began the book by stating, "One of the most important principles that the forthcoming Islamic government, as well as the Islamic movement, must adhere to, is the condition of nonviolence."[7] Citing prophetic tradition, al-Shirazi related a saying that "violence is a part of the army of ignorance"—that is, the party of unbelief and deviation.

Examining nonviolence in further detail, al-Shirazi divided the subject into three specific categories: nonviolence by nature, nonviolence by coercion, and nonviolence by design. He gave primacy to the first category, stating that "in addition to reaching the pleasant goal that will be characterized by continual existence, nonviolence is a virtue that comforts the soul."[8] Nonviolence "by nature" refers to the cultivation of a refined character through virtuous discipline, which is achieved through "substantial and, very often, strenuous psychological and character forming education and training."[9] This, of course, fundamentally differs from practicing nonviolence out of weakness ("by coercion") or out of strategic considerations ("by design"). Finding ample support in the Qur'an, al-Shirazi also related several traditions from the Prophet Muhammad and the Holy Imams that reinforce this particular conception of nonviolence and infuse it with sacred status. One example states:

The Messenger of God is quoted as saying: "Shall I inform you of the best morals of this world and the hereafter? (They are) to forgive he who oppresses you, to make a bond with he who severs from you, to be kind to he who insults you, and to give to he who deprives you."[10]

The "weapon" of nonviolence, al-Shirazi argued, "is more effective than the weapon of violence, just as the soul is stronger than the body, so too is non-violence, since it is the weapon of the soul, and so it is more powerful than the weapon of the body which is made of matter."[11] Nonviolence, he further writes, is "a weapon that attracts the hearts and minds to one who advocates it, and incites the people against his adversaries."[12] This aspect of nonviolence is personified in the aforementioned stories of the Prophet's companions Bilal, Sumayya, and Amar, among others. The lives of God's prophets throughout human history are also filled with examples that reveal the righteous power of the weapon of non-violence. Shirazi writes that "the nonviolence of the prophet Abraham defeated King Nimrod's violence, and Moses' nonviolence defeated Pharaoh's violence, and Jesus' nonviolence defeated Herod's violence, and the nonviolence of the Messenger of God [i.e., Muhammad] defeated the violence of the pagans' great knights."[13] These prophetic models, he asserts, reinforce the idea that nonvio-lence must be built on the foundation of a strong, patient, and resilient character, capable of putting "things right, whether constructive or destructive, with total leniency so that no one is harmed by the cure."[14]

In response to critics and skeptics of Islamic nonviolence who may point to the wars that the Prophet Muhammad once fought in Medina or the military campaigns waged by his successors such as Imam Ali, al-Shirazi argues that those cases were the "lesser of two evils," comparing them to "when a patient reluctantly agrees to undergo a surgical operation to amputate a limb in order to prevent greater harm to his body and health."[15] Explaining this qualification fur-ther, al-Shirazi articulates a view that resembles just war theory. He states, "If the Messenger of God had ignored the pagans and their mischievous deeds and had left them to their own accords, that would have resulted in the loss of thousands, if not millions, of lives, whereas the given response of the Messenger of God lim-ited it to less than fourteen-hundred."[16] This concession, however, does not lead al-Shirazi to concede or retract his commitment to nonviolence in modern times. It is more important now than ever. Rather, he asserts that nonviolence is more than simply nonaggression; it means that "an individual would not attempt to hurt another individual, even with respect to the strongest of his adversaries and even if he had the right to do so; [for] Allah the Almighty states [in the Qur'an]: 'And if you forgive, it is closest to righteousness.'"[17]

In modern times warfare and weaponry have reached horrific new heights, most notably in the form of the atomic bomb. "The world witnesses in the modern age," wrote al-Shirazi, "the worst forms of killing, torture, and burning and the degradation of the nobility of the human being."[18] The destructive capabilities of the modern age are so great that al-Shirazi denounced nuclear weapons, weapons of mass destruction, and other "advanced weaponry" altogether and (perhaps unrealistically) counseled that humanity should return to "light" and "primitive arms" for use only in case of extreme emergency. He stated, "There should be committees to change the advanced weapons into light weapons like the rifle, then to substitute these light weapons for primitive weapons like the sword and the spear, for it is a grave error for humanity to prepare weapons which will annihilate both the fighter and his enemy."[19]

Thus far, I have focused on what al-Shirazi referred to as the enactment of "physical nonviolence," but there are two other forms worthy of attention. Al-Shirazi described the enactment of "verbal nonviolence" and "nonviolence of the heart" as well. The latter is described in terms of traditional Islamic discourses on *jihad al-nafs*, or "jihad of the self (or soul)." According to al-Shirazi, these forms of nonviolence are more difficult to implement than "physical nonviolence" but must be practiced nonetheless. "Verbal nonviolence," as he defined it, "is to curb one's tongue and check one's words in order to make sure one's words do not damage the aggressor, whether his aggression was physical or verbal."[20] Hostile and aggressive speech is easily enacted and may escape retribution, unrestrained by threats of physical violence, and therefore a believer must restrain his or her tongue simply out of virtue. Therefore, al-Shirazi called on believers who are faced with an onslaught of insults and accusations to "seek refuge in silence and abstain from responding likewise, in the interest of the cause and progress of Islam."[21] After all, the Qur'an states, "Respond [to evil] with what is better, so that those between whom there was enmity shall become like affectionate friends."[22]

The last form of nonviolence described by al-Shirazi, "nonviolence of the heart," is when "one does not fill his heart with violence towards foes and adversaries." This is the most difficult form of nonviolence. For so long as violence lingers in the heart, "it is inevitable that this violence will come to the surface, even if under unusual circumstances."[23] The Prophet Muhammad reportedly said, "If a person's heart is healthy, his body will be in comfort, and if the heart is malicious, the body will be malevolent."[24] Imam Ali also reportedly said, "The weapon of evil is hatred" and "he who abandons hatred will have a relieved heart."[25] In the eighth century, the sixth imam, Jafar al-Sadiq further said that "he whose heart is hard is distant from his Lord."[26] Al-Shirazi therefore counseled people to purify their hearts by undertaking jihad al-nafs, also known as "the greater jihad" (*jihad al-akbar*). "Such qualities," he wrote, "require such determined self-training and practice that are no less difficult than the hardships and dangers of the battlefields."[27]

Persecution and Politics

The Iraqi branch of the Baathist Party, a pan-Arab socialist party originating in Syria, took control of Iraq through a military coup in 1968. The coup followed years of internal political conflict after the downfall of the British-installed Hashemite monarchy in 1958. The Baathist leadership in Iraq consisted primarily of nominally Sunni Arabs, a minority in a country that was dominated by Shi'ite Arabs and had a Kurdish majority in the north. In 1969 al-Shirazi's elder brother, Hassan, was imprisoned in Baghdad by the Baathist regime and tortured, forcing him to flee to Lebanon where he was assassinated by Iraqi agents in Beirut. Hassan had written a series of poems mocking the Iraqi regime and openly denouncing the ruling Baathists as thugs and gangsters.[28] In 1970 the Baathist regime claimed it had discovered a plot to overthrow Iraq that had been inspired by neighboring Iran, and it served as a pretext for a purge of the regime's internal opponents, including religious associations. Numerous "Iranians" (i.e., Shi'ite clerics) residing in Iraq were expelled.[29] In 1971 Muhammad al-Shirazi and his family escaped persecution in Iraq—possibly execution—by fleeing to the small and wealthy kingdom of Kuwait under cover of night.

The Iranian Revolution of Grand Ayatollah Ruhullah Khomeini, which deposed the U.S.-backed shah in 1979, led al-Shirazi to leave Kuwait and move to the Shi'ite holy city of Qom in Iran. That same year, Saddam Hussein, a nominally Sunni Baathist, ascended to power in Iraq and succeeded his kinsman Gen. Ahmed Hasan al-Bakr as its authoritarian president. Longstanding territorial disputes between Iraq and Iran soon grew into full-scale war amid the shifts in power, and Sunni-Shi'ite tensions were exacerbated for political ends.

At the start of the Iranian Revolution, Khomeini and his followers concealed their true intentions, claiming that neither he nor the Shi'ite clergy would hold direct power. Khomeini even allegedly stated that he had abandoned his innovative doctrine of *velayat-e faqih* (guardianship of the jurist).[30] But as events in Iran evolved, the clerical factions rose to dominance, outmaneuvering and purging Iranian leftists and others, and implemented a program that monopolized power in the hands of the Shi'ite clergy and their institutions.[31] Khomeini's doctrine of velayat-e faqih became the basis of the revolutionary Islamic republic.

These developments drew opposition from al-Shirazi for a number of reasons. Not long after his arrival in Qom, he expressed his reservations about Khomeini's conception of Islamic governance, namely the idea of rule by a single cleric as supreme leader. Al-Shirazi instead advocated a government led by a *shurat al-fuqaha* ("council of jurists") in place of Khomeini's velayat-e faqih, because he believed it would prevent the creation of a dictatorship.[32] For al-Shirazi the most authoritative clerics were peers to one another, and he opposed the subordination of the other grand ayatollahs to a single cleric. He therefore turned down positions in the Iranian government and focused his attention on the Islamic seminary in Qom, providing social services and expanding his popular following, largely through a network of *husayniyyas*, which are religious lodges associated with the rituals of Ashura. However, when al-Shirazi publicly expressed his opposition to the ongoing Iran-Iraq War (1980–1988) and criticized the regime's execution of political opponents and confiscation of property, the regime exerted increasing pressure and persecution of his supporters, known as the *Shiraziyyin*.

During the 1990s after the death of Khomeini, al-Shirazi's followers were subjected to persecution, arrest, and torture by the Iranian regime and its most zealous supporters. Al-Shirazi refused to recognize the supreme leadership of Khomeini's successor, Hojjat al-Islam (later Ayatollah) Ali Khamenei, a former president of Iran and head of the Islamic Revolutionary Guard Corps. He continued to press for a democratic consultative system of clerical leadership to lead Iran. Khamenei, in fact, lacked the religious credentials to hold the high office, and revisions to the constitution of the Islamic Republic were made to facilitate his rule. In 1995 Khamenei traveled to Qom in order to meet with its esteemed clerics, but al-Shirazi refused to see him. The following year al-Shirazi's two sons, both proponents of their father's ideas, were arrested and tortured in Iran.[33]

One book, *Aspects of the Political Theory of Imam Muhammad Shirazi*, details al-Shirazi's conception of Islamic governance as a rival to the Iranian regime's system of velayat-e faqih. Its author, Muhammad G. Ayub, provides an analysis of al-Shirazi's writings from his voluminous fiqh series and includes extensive translations from his compiled statements on the subject. Ayub details how al-Shirazi held freedom to be the fundamental nature of humanity, and how he believed the relationship between freedom and the oneness of God (tawhid) was essential because it frees humanity from servitude to other men, such as kings (e.g., the shah).[34] This freedom includes the right to organize political parties and engage in political action. "The state has no right to forbid mass-meetings or gatherings, whether temporary for celebration, condolences, or exchange of views; or permanent, as in the case of forming societies, trade unions, committees and the like," al-Shirazi wrote, "because of the fundamental nature of human freedom."[35] The leadership of such bodies must be elected by the masses through consultation (*shura*), for "all the party's institutions and members must be one with the masses, channeling their energies and leading them in the battles of liberation from colonialism and oppression."[36] Revolutions, furthermore, are only legitimate if they are social in nature, reflecting the will of the people. Military coups are illegitimate, because possession of arms and weaponry does not qualify one group for guardianship over another, including a nation.[37] A true revolution, al-Shirazi asserted, will bring about "a new social and political life abundant with hope, optimism and giving, but only if the masses are well aware of the role they have to play, and if they do not allow a small faction to steal the revolution and liquidate others."[38]

Just as freedom is part of the fundamental nature of humanity, violence is an abnormality that brings about coercion, dictatorship, and war. The masses must "embody peace in their thought, words, and actions, towards both friends and foes."[39] According to al-Shirazi, the objectives of the people in the cause of a social revolution must be achieved through peaceful means. He compared resorting to violence to "eating a dead animal's carcass out of desperate necessity."[40] Consumption of carrion is forbidden in the Qur'an but permitted to Muslims if faced with starvation. It states:

> [God] has only forbidden you carrion and blood and the flesh of swine and that over which any other name has been invoked other than God. But whoever is forced out of necessity (to eat of them), without willful disobedience, then no sin is upon him. Verily God is Forgiving, Compassionate.[41]

Muslims must therefore work toward averting such dire circumstances by stopping the arms race, avoiding military coups, reforming the United Nations, and spreading social justice throughout the world, according to al-Shirazi.[42] Muslims should furthermore avert war in every possible way, for even when fighting ceases, people never forget those who killed their families and neighbors.[43] Peace, in fact, is the overall framework of the Islamic state, contrary to those groups like the Iranian regime or the Taliban who operate nation-states on the basis of force, coercion, and intimidation.

Beyond Death

After years of house arrest in Qom, al-Shirazi died suddenly of a stroke in December 2001. Many of his followers believed that he was actually assassinated—likely poisoned—by Khamenei's regime. These allegations have assumed the form of conspiracy theories that fit into existing Shi'ite narratives about the martyrdoms of the Holy Imams (most of whom were allegedly poisoned) at the hands of tyrannical illegitimate rulers. Such beliefs were further strengthened by the Iranian regime's shocking conduct following al-Shirazi's death. As the massive funeral procession for al-Shirazi traveled through the streets of Qom, Iranian security forces in camouflage uniforms attacked the pallbearers and stole al-Shirazi's corpse—which fell to the street twice during the chaos—before they whisked it away into a waiting minibus.[44] Images of the scene later made it onto the Internet, despite a media blackout in Iran. In defiance of al-Shirazi's own burial wishes, the regime's security forces buried his body in the Hazrat Fatemah al-Massoumeh Shrine in Qom without the presence of his family or its permission.[45] The grave is nondescript, difficult to reach, and monitored by the state security forces. In 2005 it was reported that a group of women from al-Shirazi's family, including his own daughters, were praying at his grave when they were beaten and arrested.[46] Since his death, al-Shirazi's followers have bestowed the revered title of "imam" and even *mujaddid* (renewer of the faith) on him, drawing the ire of religious outsiders. The modest, monastic room in Qom where al-Shirazi once lived has been turned into a shrine of sorts, where visitors can come and take photographs of his turban and his simple mattress lying on a bare floor.[47]

Today the Shiraziyyin exist throughout the entire Gulf region and even in Western countries such as the United States, to which many have fled from persecution in countries such as Iran and Iraq. The spiritual center or capital of the Shiraziyyin, however, remains at Karbala. In fact, the connection between Karbala and the Shiraziyyin is still so strong that they are commonly known to outsiders as the *Jama'at Karbala*, or the "Karbala Group."[48] Perhaps because of their strong identity with Karbala, where Imam Husayn was martyred, the Shiraziyyin have shown a strong ability to persevere in hostile environments.[49] For example, they form the largest Shi'ite movement in Sunni-Wahhabite Saudi Arabia, under the leadership of Shaykh Hasan al-Saffar, an activist and proponent of sectarian reconciliation and democracy.

Meanwhile, Shirazi's younger brother, Grand Ayatollah Sadiq Hussaini al-Shirazi, has assumed the role of marja al-taqlid and the global leadership of the Shiraziyyin, leading the hawza in Qom and guiding the group in their struggles with their enemies, such as the Dawah Party. The six sons of Muhammad al-Shirazi and four sons of Sadiq al-Shirazi are also mujtahids and play an important role in spreading the teachings of the group, especially through the Internet and new media.[50] The masses may lack the personal charismatic virtues of al-Shirazi, but their continuing devotion to his teachings is unquestionable. In a speech given the day after Muhammad al-Shirazi's funeral, Sadiq consoled the crowd of heartbroken mourners by stating, "We should resolve, and in our resolution make a bond and a promise to Allah Almighty, that we would continue his path in all that we have learnt from him or shall learn from his heritage in the future."[51]

8

The Ascetic

The Qur'an does not condone monasticism. It relates that Allah never asked people to undertake such extreme forms of piety, stating, "But monasticism, which they invented, We [i.e., Allah] did not prescribe it for them" (57:27). Instead, the Qur'an and sunna of the Prophet Muhammad counsel Muslims to adhere to a form of moderate asceticism described in Islamic tradition as the "middle path." India, home of one of the largest Muslim populations in the world, has a long-standing tradition of asceticism and monasticism, evident in the South Asian traditions of Hinduism, Buddhism, and Jainism. The moderate asceticism advocated by Islam is certainly less withdrawn from the world than the asceticism found in these indigenous Indian traditions, which Muslims personally encountered when they arrived in the early eighth century. Nevertheless, the otherworldly piety of Muslim holy men and women, most notably among the Sufis, was something readily understood in the religious climate of the region.

The Muslim scholar, preacher of nonviolence, and vegetarian Wahiduddin Khan is a modern example of India's Muslim holy men who embody the "middle path" of Islam. Often seen dressed in a simple white robe, accented by his shaggy yet flowing grey beard and a large pair of black-rimmed glasses, Maulana (meaning "respected scholar," or literally "our master") Wahiduddin Khan visibly reflects the message that he teaches to his followers. A popular writer, speaker, and recipient of numerous humanitarian awards in India and abroad, he is a vocal champion of spiritual reform and nonviolence in Islam, actively engaged in what he calls the "true jihad."

The Early Years

Wahiduddin Khan was born in the village of Badharia near Azamgarh in northern India in January 1925, when the British Empire still ruled the subcontinent. The northern regions of India have always been the stronghold of Indian Islam, centered around the city of Delhi, which was once the capital of numerous Muslim Sultanates on the subcontinent. Muslims of every sect and sort settled among India's seemingly infinite variety of religionists, including legalistic Sunnis, Ismailis, Ahmadiyyas, Twelver Shi'ites, and enraptured Sufi mystics. As a boy, Wahiduddin lost his father in 1929, leaving him to be raised by his mother and his uncle, who guided Wahiduddin's education in his stead.[1] His family was deeply involved in the Indian nationalist movement associated with the Indian National Congress seeking freedom and independence from British rule. Influenced by these nationalist circles, his brother and cousins were educated in modern, Western-style schools. Wahiduddin, however, received an Islamic education and enrolled as a student at the Madrasatul Islah in 1938, an institution (founded in 1908) near Azamgarh that was devoted to the reform and revival of Islam. Wahiduddin studied at the reformist madrassa for six years, focusing on the study of the Qur'an and its conception of nature, before graduating in 1944.[2]

Although respected in religious circles, his Islamic education left him unprepared to deal with colleagues and critics who had received Western-style secular educations, including his own family members, which troubled him and shook his belief in Islam. But never one to back down from a challenge, Wahiduddin committed himself to the study of Arabic to examine Islamic sources in the original and English to study modern science and philosophy, including the writings of figures such as Karl Marx and Bertrand Russell, spending long hours in a library.[3] This rigorous personal study ultimately renewed his faith in Islam and equipped him for the challenges that lay ahead.

After the partition of India in 1947, Wahiduddin remained in northern India, as did millions of other Muslims, and did not undertake the treacherous migration to the new Muslim state of Pakistan. Instead, he was committed to the preservation of the Muslim community in Hindu-majority India and involved himself in Sunni Islamist activist circles, joining the Indian branch of Abu Ala Mawdudi's Jamaat-i Islami in 1949. As an Islamic scholar, he quickly moved up the leadership ranks of the branch, called the Jamaat-i Islami Hind, and assumed control of the group's publishing house in Rampur, often writing for the Jamaat's official journal.[4]

The Jamaat-i Islami had been founded in Lahore in August 1941 as a platform for Mawdudi, a journalist by trade, to promote his radical vision of an Islamic state.[5] The new ideological perspective offered by the Jamaat was presented as "true Islam," and traditional ulama and Sufi pirs were the targets of the group's criticism and rebuke.[6] The Jamaat sought to transform secular Pakistan into a state based on the sovereignty of God (*al-hakimiyya*), which meant the full implementation of Islamic law (sharia) to replace idolatrous "man-made" systems. Some members of the group even advocated violent revolution as a means to this end. This was not the method publicly adopted by the leadership of the organization, though, which stressed instead the use of legal, constitutional channels for reforming Pakistan along Islamist lines. Nevertheless, the Jamaat's activities were considered subversive, and it was frequently faced with government suppression. Meanwhile in India, the Jamaat-i Islami Hind, headquartered in Rampur at the time, focused its efforts on social services, advocacy, and Islamic propagation (dawa) aimed at the eventual Islamization of Hindu-majority India.

During his time in the Jamaat-i Islami Hind, Wahiduddin Khan published his first book, *Naye Ahd Ke Darwaze Par* (*On the Threshold of a New Era*), in Urdu in 1955. In it he presented his reformist vision of modern Islam for the first time. The book was followed by a second, more elaborate treatise titled *Ilme Jadid Ka Challenge* (*Islam and Modern Challenges*), better known by the title *God Arises*, which was later adopted by several Arab universities under the title *al-Islam Yatahadda* and translated into languages including English, Arabic, Malay, Hindi, and Turkish.[7] *God Arises* is a thoroughly modernist rendering of Islam, arguing that the message of the Qur'an is entirely in harmony with the findings of modern science. "Today," Wahiduddin writes, "that very same weapon—science—which was supposed to have brought religion to an ignominious end, has at last been turned against the scoffers and atheists, and we are, at the moment, witnessing the same momentous revolution in thinking that took place in the seventh century with the advent of the Prophet of Islam."[8] The advances of science, he further notes, have forced scholars of religion to reexamine the claims and tenets of their religions, including the notion that creation was the product of a godhead. "I am convinced that, far from having a damaging effect on religion," he writes, "modern knowledge has served to clarify and consolidate its truths."[9]

In the process of traversing a range of scientific subject areas throughout the book, including physics, geology, and biology, Wahiduddin frequently turns to the subject of political systems and critiques the dominant Western ideologies of the day. These are the areas where his affiliation with Islamism at the time becomes most evident. For instance, he writes that "in both democratic and despotic systems, human equality has remained an unattainable ideal, for power has always had to be put in the hands of a few individuals, with others becoming their subjects; this disparity can only disappear when God is considered sovereign."[10] Such ideas clearly reflect Abu Ala Mawdudi's conception of al-hakimiyya, which was also adopted by the Egyptian Islamist Sayyid Qutb in his own writings, such as the controversial book *Milestones*. Wahiduddin's use of the concept, however, lacks the revolutionary zeal of Mawdudi or Qutb, seeking instead to articulate a holistic vision of Islamic society that offers practical social benefits and safeguards. He was far more interested in the social activism and organizational structure of the Jamaat than Mawdudi's actual ideological vision.[11]

A New Direction

In time Wahiduddin emerged as a prominent critic of Mawdudi's Islamist ideas, which he saw as reactionary rather than authentically Islamic and abandoned the Jamaat and its political agenda in 1962. From Wahiduddin's perspective, Mawdudi was treating politics as the center of Islamic activity, when tawhid (the oneness of God) is the actual heart of Islam and the call (dawa) to tawhid should be the center of all Islamic activity, making all else, including politics and economics, secondary.[12] This break with the Islamists led Wahiduddin to gravitate toward another influential Muslim group, the Tablighi Jamaat, because it emphasized Islamic spirituality and political quietism. The Tablighi Jamaat was established in 1927 by Maulana Muhammad Ilyas in the Mewat region south of Delhi as an apolitical movement emphasizing Muslim personal renewal through "reverting" to the ways (sunna) of the Prophet Muhammad.[13] Wahiduddin was, however, still interested in making Islam relevant to the modern age and grew disillusioned with the Tablighi's archtraditionalism, rejection of *ijtihad* (creative rethinking), and perceived backwardness, ultimately leaving the organization in 1975.[14] This break motivated Wahiduddin to establish his own organization, the Islamic Center at New Delhi, which quickly began to publish in Urdu a monthly Islamic journal called *al-Risala*, followed later by editions in English and Hindi, to freely express Wahiduddin's ideas, including his views on nonviolence.

Wahiduddin's conception of nonviolence is perhaps best articulated in his treatise *Islam and Peace*. Growing up at the height of India's independence movement, Wahiduddin held great admiration for Mohandas Gandhi and expressed these sentiments in his book. For instance, he writes, "Our greatest need is to fulfill Mahatma Gandhi's mission . . . after political change we have to bring about social change in our country through Gandhi Andolan, that is, a nonviolent movement."[15] Nonviolence, he states, begins in the mind of an individual, which is the basic unit of human society, and must be cultivated through a long and laborious struggle.[16] This struggle (jihad) consists of many levels, but the most important is education and the development of the mind. He writes that "to make a nonviolent world for a peaceful society, there is only one way, and that is by using educative method[s] to convert people's thinking from violence to nonviolence, and to enable them to see the solution to matters of controversy through peaceful means" and that "it is from such intellectual awareness alone that a nonviolent world and a peaceful society can be constructed."[17] Nonviolence, he assures his readers, is completely in keeping with the teachings of the Qur'an. Pointing to chapter 2, verse 205, Wahiduddin states that God does not love *fasad*, a term he interprets to mean violence, or any action that "results in disruption of the social system, causing huge losses in terms of lives and property."[18] He also refers his readers to the Qur'an's emphasis on patience (*sabr*) above any other virtue, noting that "patience implies a peaceful response or reaction, whereas impatience implies a violent response."[19] The Qur'anic concept of jihad, he further argues, also refers to nonviolence:

Jihad means struggle, to struggle one's utmost. It must be appreciated at the outset that this word is used for nonviolent struggle as opposed to violent struggle. One clear proof of this is the verse of the Qur'an (25:52) which says: 'Perform jihad with this (i.e., the word of the Qur'an) most strenuously.' The Qur'an is not a sword or a gun. It is a book of ideology. In such a case, performing jihad with the Qur'an would mean an ideological struggle to conquer peoples' hearts and minds through Islam's superior philosophy.[20]

Wahiduddin contrasts his reading of jihad as nonviolent activism with the term qital, which is described as violent activism. Jihad, which awakens the conscience and overcomes the human ego, is marked by positive values, friendship, construction, and life, while qital is driven by the ego and embroils people in problems, destruction, and death.[21]

Wahiduddin supports his reading of the Qur'an by referring to the life of the Prophet Muhammad. Unlike most of the proponents of Islamic nonviolence, Wahiduddin does not emphasize the primacy of the Meccan period over the Medinan period. In fact, he points to an event at the height of the Medinan period when Muhammad was embroiled in warfare against the pagan Meccans. In 628 Muhammad signed a peace treaty with the Meccans, known as the Treaty of Hudaybiyya. The treaty was established at a time of great tension when Muhammad and a thousand Muslims had traveled unarmed to pagan-ruled Mecca on pilgrimage.[22] The treaty stipulated that fighting between the Muslims and the Meccans would cease for a period of ten years, even though many of the Muslims found the terms of the treaty disagreeable, including the stipulation that called for the return of some Muslim refugees to Mecca.[23] Nevertheless, Muslim tradition has treated this event as a triumph for Islam. "Hudaybiyya," Wahiduddin asserts, "symbolizes the greatness of the power of peace against the power of war."[24] The peace treaty, he argues, "enabled the energies of the believers to be utilized in peaceful constructive activities instead of being dissipated in a futile armed encounter."[25] Among the events that occurred then, Muslim tradition relates that Muhammad sent letters to the great rulers of the time, including Heraclius, emperor of Byzantium, and Chosroes, the shah of Sasanian Persia, inviting them to embrace Islam (i.e., dawa).[26]

More importantly, however, the Treaty of Hudaybiyya meant that the Muslims could freely interact with their opponents in Mecca and Islam's missionary message could be conveyed into the heart of hostile pagan territory.[27] "The peace treaty," Wahiduddin explains, "cleared the path for the direct propagation of Islam [and] the opponents came to accept Islam in such great numbers, so that ultimately, by numerical power alone, Islam became the victor."[28] This development ultimately allowed the Muslim conquest of Mecca in 630 (after the treaty was violated by a Meccan ally) to occur without open combat, and Muhammad granted clemency to the city's pagan inhabitants, who were once the most bitter and cruel enemies of Islam.

Confronting Atrocities

Stemming from his interpretations of the Qur'an and the life of the Prophet Muhammad, Wahiduddin rejects the "dichotomous thinking" found among many modern Muslims that divides the world into those who support Islam and those who seem to be its enemies. He notes that because "Western civilization does not appear to them to be friendly to Islam, they tend to regard it as an enemy of Islam."[29] Instead Wahiduddin points to an important third category where the latent potential for dawa resides. If Muslims were to extricate themselves from their "rigid pattern of thought," they would see that the West actually falls into a category driven by economic interests and competition rather than actual enmity for Islam.[30] The extremist narrative of violence, of course, disputes such a claim and articulates the very sort of dichotomy that Wahiduddin explicitly rejects.

Wahiduddin supports his view by invoking a dark and tragic event in Islamic history, a terrible time when innumerable Muslims perished. He refers to the Mongol invasion of the thirteenth century, when the great Abbasid city of Baghdad was laid to waste and gruesome towers of human heads were left behind. The once powerful Muslims were conquered by the brutal force and superior armies of the pagan Mongols (Tartars), who swept through the heartlands of the Muslim world from the east. Through these tragic events, the Mongols became overt enemies of Islam. Yet, referring to the years that followed, when the Mongol rulers such as Ghazan Khan eventually converted to Islam, Wahiduddin notes that the Muslims "re-channeled their energies by silently engaging themselves in peaceful dawa work among the victorious Tartars," and this dawa "verified the dictum of the Qur'an (in verse 41:34) that, through dawa, the opponents of Islam would become its supporters and friends."[31] This view clearly has important implications for Muslims living in Hindu-majority India. The ideals of nonviolence and peaceful activism have frequently been put to the test there, where communal violence has remained tragically commonplace since the time of the partition.

One of the most tragic incidents in the history of Indian Islam occurred in 1992 when a massive crowd of Hindu extremists attacked and destroyed the Babri Mosque (built in 1528) in the northern town of Ayodhya to build a temple devoted to the god Rama on the site. The destruction of the mosque prompted nationwide rioting between Hindus and Muslims where more than two thousand people died and numerous other atrocities occurred.[32] In Mumbai, for example, it was reported that men were stopped in the streets by Hindu mobs, forced to pull down their pants, and, if they were circumcised (as are Muslim men), they were stabbed. Women were gang-raped.[33] Such horrific incidents obviously present a challenge for proponents of nonviolence seeking to persuade others to embrace their path.

In the aftermath of the riots, Wahiduddin Khan addressed the tragedy through his official journal, *al-Risala*. The actions and slogans of the extremists, he wrote, were "undeniably against the teachings of the father of the nation, Mahatma Gandhi, and, if not immediately rectified, will plunge the country into total destruction."[34] As a solution to the conflict, he offered a three-point plan to bring about national reconciliation: (1) Muslims would give up any plan to rebuild the Babri Mosque; (2) Hindus would give up any demands on any other Muslim religious sites; and (3) the Indian constitution would be amended to ensure that the status of all places of worship, other than Ayodhya, could not be changed.[35] The proposal was accompanied by an organized fifteen-day peace march. Wahiduddin marched alongside a Jain leader, Acharya Muni Sushil Kumar, and a Hindu guru, Swami Chidanand Saraswati, addressing large crowds at thirty-five locations from Mumbai to Nagpur about interfaith harmony.[36] The campaign did much to ease tensions at the time.

The shocking violence of the riots, however, still presented challenges to nonviolence that had to be addressed. As he acknowledged the "sacrifices" that Muslims had made and that the violence had "claimed more Muslim lives than the number of stones used in the mosque's construction," Wahiduddin never wavered in his commitment to nonviolence.[37] Furthermore, he completely refrained from lashing out against the Hindu majority and argued instead that the demolition of the mosque had been purely political in nature and not a matter of religious intolerance, thus absolving Hindus as a whole of the blame. He further stressed that violence and cyclical retribution would have dire implications for all of India, including terrible economic implications that would harm the entire country's future. "The present generation of India," he wrote, "has to decide what kind of India it is going to bequeath to the coming generation—an advanced, prosperous India, or a poor, ruined India, unfit to be inhabited, by Hindus, Muslims or any other person."[38]

To foster a prosperous future for Muslims and all others in India, Wahiduddin insisted that education (and the resources to provide it) is absolutely essential. Society as a whole, he argued, must use the power of education to transform the way people think about their problems and enable them to seek the solution to matters through peaceful means.[39] Challenges and conflicts can actually serve as catalysts for human progress, so long as the responses to those challenges are nonviolent and motivate greater education and innovation to meet the tests at hand. The violence and suffering that Muslims have experienced, Wahiduddin further rationalized, may even be the result of God's wrath for their failure to be, as the Qur'an puts it (3:110), the "best community raised up from humanity."[40] The Muslims must take their own destiny into their hands.

The political groups associated with the violence at Ayodhya, Gujarat, and other places, included the Bharatiya Janata Party, Rashtriya Swayamsevak Sangh (RSS), and Vishva Hindu Parishad. The aggressive anti-Muslim sentiment found in these Hindu groups is well known and alarming.[41] Therefore, it would certainly be understandable if Wahiduddin shunned such groups. Many in India's Muslim minority feel cloistered and besieged because of the rise of militant Hindu ultranationalism (i.e., Hindutva). Some Muslims have even called for violence and armed conflict as a means to defend their communities against the groups. Wahiduddin, however, has rejected such calls and responded by quoting the Qur'an that "no one despairs of God's mercy except those who have no faith" (12:87), and he has met directly with the leaders of the RSS and other anti-Muslim Hindu groups. In his view, Muslims must interact with those who oppose them in order to demonstrate the true teachings of Islam (a form of dawa) and create dialogue to show that

Muslims are useful allies for the progress of society. For this reason, some in the Muslim community have seen Wahiduddin as a traitor and dubbed him the "RSS Maulana."[42] Gandhi, of course, experienced similar criticism from certain Hindus in India, as did King from segments of the African American community.

Toward the Future

For his many efforts at promoting peace and nonviolence, Wahiduddin Khan has received numerous accolades, most recently the 2010 Rajiv Gandhi National Sadbhavana Award in India. He previously received the Demiurgus Peace International Award from the Nuclear Disarmament Forum in Zug, Switzerland, among several other international and national awards.[43] Now in his eighties, Wahiduddin has produced some two hundred books in his lifetime, many of which have been translated into multiple languages. In the meantime, he has continued to lecture and teach throughout the world at Islamic and interfaith conferences designed to foster dialogue and peaceful relations among nations and communities. Promoting reconciliation between India and Pakistan, in particular, has been one of his top priorities. Many of these interfaith events have been organized by the nonprofit Centre for Peace and Spirituality (CPS), which Wahiduddin Khan founded in January of 2001 in New Delhi. The stated mission of the center is a bold and ambitious one, as it aims to "cause the message of peace and spirituality to enter each and every home of the world, in order to usher in an era of global peace and unity."[44]

Maulana Wahiduddin Khan embodies what Muslims traditionally call a *zahid* in Arabic. The term refers to a person who renounces or withdraws from worldly things. This designation is appropriate not only in reference to Wahiduddin's ascetic piety, but perhaps more so for his renunciation of violence. For Wahiduddin, Islam offers the world an ideology of peace. Islam, he teaches, always seeks a state of peace, because all that Islam aims to create—spiritual progress, intellectual development, character building, social reform, education, and above all missionary work (dawa)—can only be achieved in an atmosphere of peace and harmony. Every teaching in Islam, he asserts, is based on the principle of peace, and any deviation from that principle is a deviation from Islam.[45] For, as the Qur'an states, "God guides all who seek His favor to the paths of peace and leads them out of the darkness into the light" (5:16).

9

Microfinance

In the popular 1993 song, "Keep Ya Head Up," the late African American poet Tupac Amaru Shakur, observed, "They have money for wars, but can't feed the poor." One need only look at the world's total annual military expenditures, over one trillion dollars, to truly see the extent of that simple yet disturbing observation. The wealth of the world is concentrated in a very small percentage of the global population controlled by certain power structures. The United States is the wealthiest country on earth, and its largest city, New York City, alone is home to sixty billionaires.[1] The U.S. government has an annual military budget of some $600 billion, and yet poverty and unemployment remain widespread in the land of opportunity.[2] Even more egregious are the developing nations, such as North Korea, that continue to funnel huge amounts of their limited wealth and resources toward their militaries while their people struggle in extreme poverty and even face starvation.

Proponents of the narrative of violence have offered no solutions to economic depression and underdevelopment, aside from claiming the wealth of their victims as booty. The false consciousness evident in their words and actions only worsens the conditions of daily life for their people. Imagine, for instance, what Osama bin Laden might have done if he had used his great personal wealth to build proper schools, wells, and health clinics, instead of funding terrorist camps and arms? In contrast, the narrative of nonviolence proposes that when the means used by those in power to maintain their dominance are exposed as unjustified, the subsequent loss of prestige will cause the power structure to falter, and the conditions of the community can be reformed justly, according to the popular will and means of the community. These reforms include the reallocation of resources, previously channeled toward outlets such as exorbitant military expenditures and post-conflict reconstruction, to programs that can alleviate poverty and foster innovation and entrepreneurship. Among the most alluring and rapidly growing of such economic programs is microfinance, previously referenced in chapter 3, as pioneered by figures such as Nobel laureate Muhammad Yunus of Bangladesh and American economist John Hatch.

Grameen Bank

Muhammad Yunus was born in the small village of Bathua near Chittagong on June 28, 1940, in the Bengal Province of British India (what is now Bangladesh).[3] Yunus was the third of fifteen children, and his father, Haji Muhammad Dula Meah, was a successful merchant. His mother, Sufia Khatun, was known for her generosity and greatly inspired Yunus by always helping the poor who came knocking at their door.[4] Yunus received a privileged education in his youth in Chittagong. In 1957 he began his studies at the department of economics at Dhaka University, located in the bustling capital of Bangladesh, where he completed his BA in 1960 and MA the following year. Later, while serving as a lecturer in economics at Chittagong College, he received a prestigious Fulbright scholarship to pursue his doctoral studies at Vanderbilt University in the United States. In 1969 he was awarded his PhD in economics, and he served as an assistant professor of economics at Middle Tennessee State University in Murfreesboro until 1972, when he returned to Bangladesh to serve on the faculty of Chittagong University.[5] This was a time of great suffering in his homeland; the nascent Muslim state of Pakistan had split into separate states through a devastating war.

Bangladesh's official figures say that Pakistani (i.e., West Pakistani) soldiers and pro-Pakistan militias killed an estimated 3 million people (other estimates vary), raped 200,000 women, and forced millions more to flee their homes during the nine-month War of Liberation in 1971.[6] After the war, the devastation of Bangladesh (East Pakistan) resulted in deplorable living conditions, and a terrible famine afflicted the country in 1974. Severe floods, inflation, hoarding, and outbreaks of disease produced catastrophic conditions that claimed many lives (perhaps 100,000 in the district of Rangpur alone), overwhelmingly among Bangladesh's rural poor.[7] "I found it increasingly difficult," Yunus would later recall, "to teach elegant theories of economics in the classroom while a terrible famine was raging outside."[8] Yunus decided to lead his students on a field trip to see the conditions of the people of Jobra, an impoverished village near Chittagong University.

In Jobra Yunus met a woman who survived by constructing and selling simple bamboo stools. The woman had borrowed five *taka* (the equivalent of seven cents in U.S. dollars) from a local moneylender to buy bamboo, but the loan's high interest rate and conditions (the lender could determine the stools' prices) transformed her into "a virtual slave." Deeply troubled by her story, Yunus made a list of people in the village who borrowed from the moneylenders and discovered that forty-two had borrowed a total of 856 taka, or roughly twenty-seven U.S. dollars at the time. Despite the dangers of crossing the moneylenders, he reached into his own pocket , and presented the borrowers with enough money to immediately repay their loans and free themselves from economic enslavement.[9]

Bangladesh is home to one of the largest Muslim populations in the world, and the Qur'an explicitly forbids usury and parasitic lending practices. The practice of usury, or *riba*, is condemned in the Qur'an several times, including 2:275: "Those that consume usury (riba) will not stand [on the Day of Judgment] except with those that the Satan has touched with madness." Another verse in the same chapter adds, "Oh you who believe, fear God and relinquish what remains of usury, if you are truly believers."[10] A tradition recorded in Sahih Bukhari further relates that the Prophet Muhammad was once shown the torments of Hell in a dream. After his journey through the underworld, he was informed by his two guides, the angels Gabriel and Michael, that "those you saw in the river of blood were those dealing in riba (usury)."[11] Another tradition in Sunan Abu Dawud relates that "the Apostle of God cursed the one who accepted usury, the one who paid it, the witness to it, and the one who recorded it."[12] According to Muslim jurists, Islam generally forbids profiting from another person's hardship (assuming the loan seeker is a needy person) and other acts of expropriation.[13] It is perhaps due in part to these reasons that an estimated 72 percent of people living in Muslim-majority countries do not use formal financial services.[14]

To avoid these sinful practices, alternative methods of finance that are compliant with sharia were developed over the centuries to facilitate trade and economic growth in Muslim societies. The two most common forms of sharia-compliant financing are *mudaraba* and *murabaha* loans. A mudaraba loan, also known as *qirad*, is essentially profit-sharing, such as when a bank loans money to a client (*mudarib*) in return for which the lender receives a specified percentage of the net profits of the business for a designated period. The lender and borrower also equally share the risks by jointly absorbing any loss. [15] The mudaraba model, sometimes described as the "silent partnership" model, was prominent in medieval Mediterranean trade, in part under the Italian name *commenda*.[16] This model was also common in ancient Arabia, and it has been suggested that when the Prophet Muhammad met his first wife Khadija working as her employee, he was trading with her capital in a mudaraba arrangement.[17]

The other common form of sharia-compliant loan, a murabaha loan (sometimes called a "cost-plus sale"), has a banker or lender purchase goods in his own name, sell the goods to the "borrower" with an agreed-upon price markup, and then the profit the lender derives from the sale to the client is justified simply as a service rendered. Overall, Islam does not forbid profit-taking from legitimate businesses (i.e., those that do not deal in forbidden goods, such as alcohol) as long as profits are earned and not based on any interest (*riba*) from loaning money.[18] Murabaha loans are commonly used for home financing.[19] Although interest-bearing mortgage loans and murabaha financing contracts often come close to blurring the boundaries between interest-bearing loans and credit-sale financing, Muslim jurists have nevertheless differentiated between them.[20] This type of loan has proved to be the most popular form of financing for modern Islamic banks, after banker Sami Humud modified the classical murabaha contract in the 1970s.[21]

In the impoverished Bangladeshi village of Jobra, there was an enthusiastic response to Yunus's work. Encouraged, he was motivated to expand his efforts. He began by going to all the major banks in Bangladesh and petitioning them to offer collateral-free loans to the poor so they could be free from the moneylenders. The bank managers refused, claiming that the poor were not creditworthy. The poor simply had no assets to pledge as collateral for loans. However, Yunus offered to personally become the guarantor for loans to the poor, and the banks eventually agreed. "By the middle of 1976," he recalled, "I started giving out loans to the village poor, signing all the papers the bank gave me to guarantee the loans personally and acting as a kind of informal banker on my own."[22] Yunus also devised a set of rules for his clients to follow. They would pay back their loans in small sums every week to bank officers who would travel directly to the villages. "These ideas worked," Yunus discovered. "People paid back the loans on time, every time."[23] It turned out to be a profitable business, too, but the banks still expressed reservations and prevented the expansion of Yunus's programs for collateral-free loans to the poor. Yunus decided that he would have to create a new bank. It would utilize "social collateral," where groups of borrowers are collectively responsible for repayment, and individual borrowers must vouch for (sometimes "cover") each other.[24]

The bank that Muhammad Yunus created to serve the poorest of the poor was called Grameen Bank, which means "village bank" in Bengali. Grameen Bank was unique because the owners were the borrowers themselves, and they would elect nine of the thirteen members on the board of directors. Today Grameen Bank serves the poor in every single village of Bangladesh with 8 million borrowers, 97 percent of whom are women. It also boasts an impressive repayment rate of approximately 98 percent on its loans to borrowers. When the bank first began its operations, it deliberately focused on lending to women, in part, as an act of protest against conventional banks in Bangladesh that would only lend to men.[25]

Yunus, who is the father of two daughters, recognized that women in Bangladesh were not receiving adequate opportunities and remained a largely untapped source of creativity and entrepreneurship. Initially Grameen Bank intended to have equal numbers of men and women as borrowers but quickly discovered that loans to women had a greater benefit to entire families, especially children, while men tended to keep the money for themselves.[26] "Women had more drive to overcome poverty," Yunus would later remark. Underlying these efforts was his core belief that everyone possesses enormous potential and "every human being is born into this world fully equipped not only to take care of himself or herself, but also to contribute to the well-being of the world as a whole."[27] When Yunus was coawarded the Nobel Peace Prize with Grameen Bank in 2006, the citation aptly described microfinance as a "liberating force in societies where women in particular have to struggle against repressive social and economic conditions."[28]

Although Muhammad Yunus's Grameen Bank conforms to Islamic principles, it is not, strictly speaking, compliant with normative renderings of sharia. Nevertheless, Yunus has been attentive to defending the Bank against conservative religious detractors who disapprove of its use of interest. "The purpose of the religious injunction against interest is to protect the poor from usury (riba)," he explains, "but where the poor own their own bank, the interest is in effect paid to the company they own, and therefore to themselves."[29] The same riba critique has shown up among other detractors as well. For instance, the former prime minister of Bangladesh, Sheikh Hasina, lashed out at Yunus during a speech in February 2007, referring to him implicitly as a usurer, although the speech was actually a response to Yunus's prior condemnation of political corruption in Bangladesh.[30]

Politics, both on the Left and the Right, are often simmering beneath the surface of criticisms of Grameen Bank. Critics, typically not of the religious sort, have claimed that Grameen's model is not as successful as Yunus and others suggest.[31] They point to cases where borrowers, even after initial success, fell on hard times and relapsed into poverty. Others argue that the interest rates on the microloans, typically around 20 percent annualized, are too high. Still others point to instances where the microfinance model has been overtly abused, particularly among corporate-based MFIs that have "gone public." For instance, *Business Week* and *The New Yorker* reported on microlenders in Mexico who charged outrageous interest rates between 110 and 120 percent.[32] Clearly microfinance, including the Grameen model, is not immune to human corruption or abuse and needs regulation, but this has little bearing on the underlying system itself and the potential benefits it can offer (and has offered) to impoverished and underdeveloped societies. It is not a miracle solution, but only one tool among many to help bring prosperity to the masses of human beings across the world living in substandard conditions. Although Grameen is not the focus of this chapter, it should be noted that the bank has developed a range of other MFI programs to meet the additional needs of the societies in which it works, including Grameen Telecom, a nonprofit cell-phone business that provides modern communication for rural people who never had such access.[33]

From its humble beginnings in rural Bangladesh, the Grameen Bank model has expanded across the world under the auspices of the Grameen Foundation. Led by CEO and President Alex Counts, who trained under Yunus for six years in Bangladesh, the Grameen Foundation is an independent international institution apart from the original Grameen Bank in Bangladesh, although Yunus still serves as the foundation's director emeritus.[34] In 2003 the Grameen Foundation began working in the Middle East and North Africa to create opportunities for the poor in the Arab world, especially women. In 2007 it forged an alliance with Bab Rizq Jameel Ltd. to found Grameen-Jameel Pan-Arab Microfinance Ltd. in Dubai, United Arab Emirates.[35] By 2008 Grameen-Jameel had facilitated $44 million in loans to more than 350,000 new microfinance clients through partner institutions in Egypt, Jordan, Lebanon, Morocco, Palestine, Tunisia, and Yemen.[36] As one example of the sort of projects the foundation funds, a borrower in Egypt started her own business making wooden kitchen supplies with a forty-six-dollar loan when her husband fell ill, enabling her to work from home with her three children. She credits the program with saving her family.[37]

Beyond Grameen

The Grameen Bank model of Muhammad Yunus is hardly the only microfinance program that has made an impact in the Muslim world. In 1984 American economist and Peace Corps veteran John Hatch established the aforementioned nonprofit microfinance program known as the Foundation for International Community Assistance (FINCA). Hatch's organization is credited with inventing the "village banking method" whereby neighbors come together in financial support groups called "village banks," a model that has since been widely emulated around the world.[38] According to a 2008 report, FINCA became the first microfinancing institution in Afghanistan to offer non-interest-bearing murabaha loans, beginning in 2006 as a response to market demand for loan products that are compliant with sharia. These Islamic "loans," as already discussed, are actually contracts of sale between a bank and a client.[39] Prior to the introduction of the murabaha loan program, FINCA's access to archconservative Afghanistan was highly limited, and Yunus's Grameen Bank was even expelled from the country. FINCA has since supplied loans to over ten thousand clients in Afghanistan with an average loan of \$385 dollars per client.⁴⁰ For the sake of comparison, the U.S. government spends \$6.2 million on a single M1A2 Abrams tank.⁴¹ In November 2007 FINCA further expanded its programs to the Kingdom of Jordan, where Queen Rania al-Abdullah was enlisted to serve as cochair of FINCA's village-banking campaign alongside Israeli-American actor and activist Natalie Portman.

In Jordan there are over 2.5 million refugees from Palestine and Iraq, and the nationwide labor force suffers from high unemployment, with official estimates at about 15 percent and unofficial estimates as high as 30 percent.⁴² FINCA Jordan has a head office in the capital city of Amman and operates three full branches in al-Hussein, Hitten, and Zarqa, along with four market offices in Zeziya, Deir Alla, Sahab, and Jerash. All individual loans are offered as either commercial or sharia-compliant murabaha loans, allowing clients (over 92 percent of Jordanians are Muslim) to decide which lending methodology they prefer.⁴³ At present, the FINCA program in Jordan reportedly boasts an on-time repayment rate of 99.9 percent (this exceptional rate could be inflated by rolling over loans and calling it a "repayment," but it is still alluring).⁴⁴ Queen Rania personally toured eight small businesses operated by FINCA clients in Jordan during the winter of 2008 and related that "microfinance helps unlock the productive capacities of millions around the world by giving them the means to turn a good idea into a job; it's especially effective for women, who make up the majority of the world's poor."⁴⁵ Incidentally, Queen Rania's husband, King Abdullah II, is a forty-third-generation direct descendent of the Prophet Muhammad.⁴⁶

The Aga Khan, another direct descendent of the Prophet Muhammad, has also been a leading force in bringing microfinance programs to the Muslim world. The forty-ninth hereditary imam of the Ismaili Shi'ite Muslims, the Aga Khan is the founder and chairman of the Aga Khan Development Network, which administers the Aga Khan Agency for Microfinance (AKAM). The AKAM was established in 2005 and operates in thirteen countries, including Afghanistan, Pakistan, Tajikistan, Egypt, Syria, and Mali. In January 2010 the AKAM program in Pakistan established an innovative partnership with the Pakistani postal service to provide quality microfinance services to poor populations in remote areas, especially in Sind and Punjab where there were previously no banking services for the poor.⁴⁷ In the former Soviet republic of Tajikistan, the AKAM's programs have faced an "extremely unfavorable economic environment" but still maintained strong liquidity and resiliency.[48] Meanwhile in Egypt, where 44 percent of the population lives below the poverty line, the AKAM reached nearly nineteen thousand beneficiaries in 2009, with outstanding loans of $4.5 million, and 45 percent of borrowers being women.[49]

Opponents and Criticism

Despite the widespread enthusiasm over the successes and potential of microfinance, several challenges remain that must be addressed as interest and implementation of the concept grows. As critic Jonathan Morduch has noted, "If there is one unresolved tension that animates those who spend their days working on microfinance, it entails how to navigate the trade-offs between maximizing social impact and building strong, large financial institutions."[50] Since microfinance is not a charity, MFIs must achieve self-sufficiency. If an MFI is not self-sufficient, it will shut down or rely on outside (likely state) aid or donations, in which case the MFI is not a viable effort apart from existing state welfare programs. If an MFI is not viable, it will not attract investment. At the same time, the need to achieve or preserve self-sufficiency increases risk aversion by MFIs, meaning that an MFI may not reach the poorest of the poor (presumably the goal of an MFI) because they are the riskiest clients, and thus the MFI is not eliminating poverty. It also means that interest rates are often high, so that MFIs are financially viable and able to absorb risks and losses. Some critics have proposed that interest-rate limits be imposed on MFIs, but such limits, others counter, could threaten self-sufficiency, keep investors away, and encourage the MFIs to avoid the high risks of loaning to the poorest clients. In the case of Islamic finance, it has been noted that the Muslim practice of *zakat*, or obligatory alms, "appears ideally suited to support Islamic microfinance."[51] However, more reliable and commercially viable sources of funding must be explored further, and an influx of support from the reallocation of a portion of military expenditures could help benefit these efforts.[52]

The Potential

Despite the criticism of microfinance programs, these programs have had real beneficial results in the Muslim world. This, of course, is despite the ongoing violence that plagues the peoples in countries such as Afghanistan that severely limits their potential and access to available resources. At present, even as programs have grown at an exponential rate across the world, microfinance is still in its relative infancy in the Muslim world, and tremendous potential remains on the horizon. Violence, however, threatens the potential of such tools, creating instability, endangering program staff and borrowers, disrupting trade channels, destroying essential national infrastructure such as roads and arable land, and diverting the allocation of inordinate wealth and resources to military expenditures. As U.S. president Dwight D. Eisenhower said in a 1953 speech, "Every gun that is made, every warship launched, every rocket fired signifies, in the final sense, is a theft from those who hunger and are not fed, those who are cold and are not clothed."[53] Nonviolence offers not only an effective strategy for the resolution of sociopolitical grievances, but produces the necessary climate wherein profound socioeconomic development can take place. In the following chapter, I will examine another important tool that Muslim societies can utilize to bring about greater prosperity by adopting the narrative of nonviolence—namely, the rapid expansion of women's education.

10

Women's Education

According to popular tradition, the Prophet Muhammad once said, "Seek knowledge from the cradle to the grave."[1] The statement does not specify whether the Prophet's command applies to men or women. Another saying of the Prophet clarifies the message further: "Seeking knowledge is a duty upon every Muslim male and female."[2] These sorts of prophetic traditions were apparently taken seriously throughout much of Islamic history. There are abundant records that relate the scholastic achievements of literate Muslim women in the history of Muslim societies, most notably in the science of hadith (*'ilm al-hadith*). That said, statistics from the forty-eight Muslim-majority countries in the world suggest that today in many, women remain significantly behind their male counterparts in education and even basic literacy. It would be a serious mistake, however, to take this data as evidence that a direct causal relationship exists between the lack of women's education and the religion of Islam. Rather, these differences are more broadly indicative of the developing world in general, as well as cultural mores or concerns that transcend any particular religion. Still, there is no doubt that religion, specifically Islam, has indeed been used to justify or defend misogynistic attitudes regarding the education of women, the most vivid case being the Taliban's rule in Afghanistan.

Recent studies have shown that the education of women is vital to the socioeconomic development of modern societies.[3] The mass exclusion of roughly 50 percent of a country's population from educational opportunities, and therefore much of public life in general, is profoundly debilitating to society and can undermine the future of an entire people. Such a shocking waste of human capital makes little sense in an age of rapid advancement and fierce competition among nation-states. A work force (both intellectual and labor) that is cut in half, relegating women to the status of almost total dependency, is a recipe for ongoing underdevelopment. The socioeconomic ramifications of women's exclusion from education are therefore understandably enormous for the future of modern Muslim societies.

The Big Picture

A 2005 global study conducted by the United Nations observed that secondary education is a "critical influence" on fertility and infant mortality, has a "significant beneficial effect" on health and risks for disease (including HIV/AIDS), and has a major impact (+/- 25 percent) on a country's gross national product.[4] The report also notes that "armed conflict particularly disrupts the education of girls, who may be forced to care for younger siblings as mothers become more engaged in survival and livelihood activities, or who are not allowed to go to school because of fear of rape, abduction, and sexual exploitation."[5] This observation further points to the value of adopting nonviolence for Muslim societies. Nevertheless, other important cultural barriers exist for women's education as well.

In Afghanistan, where open warfare persists, the literacy rate among women, according to an estimate by the Central Intelligence Agency (CIA) back in 2000, was already at roughly 13 percent.[6] The same report found that Afghan women on average receive only four years of schooling. In the Hashemite Kingdom of Jordan, which enjoys peace (after enduring military conflict for much of its young existence), the literacy among women is a respectable 85 percent, and females receive thirteen years of schooling on average.[7] In war-torn Somalia, the literacy rate among women, according to an estimate by the CIA from 2001, stands at roughly 26 percent.[8] The same report was unable to offer an estimate of the average years of schooling a Somali woman receives. In Egypt, where a fragile peace exists (after enduring major military and internal conflicts for much of its modern history), the literacy rate among women remains at a still troubling 60 percent.[9] (The average amount of schooling for Egyptian women is not available in the report data.) Admittedly, the statistics from these four different Muslim-majority countries provide only a sampling, but the numbers do confirm the correlations observed in the aforementioned UN report. The same correlations are generally evident in statistics collected by government agencies on infant mortality rates, family size, health, disease, and gross national product for each of these four countries. Violence, in a myriad of ways, has a devastating effect beyond the battlefield. Its broader sociopolitical and economic ramifications leave no one untouched in its wake.

Educating Women in Islam

Before proceeding any further, it is important to review some of the history of Islam and Muslim views on the education of women. Precedent is important in Islamic thought. To do this, I will review a concise selection of relevant historical and scriptural data, especially material conveyed in the form of narratives. There are several worth noting, beginning with the "Mothers of the Believers," the wives of the Prophet Muhammad during the Medinan period (622–632). These early Muslim women from the Prophet's lifetime have historically served as paradigms of Muslim femininity. The personal interaction of these women with Muhammad was unmatched, and they frequently served as personal advisers to him. Thus their reported sayings and behavior have held a significant degree of authority in Islamic thought, particularly in Sunni Islam.

In our own time, the idea of polygamy is generally treated with derision. In the tribal society of ancient Arabia, however, polygamy was commonplace, and this pre-Islamic (more broadly Semitic) practice was not introduced to Meccan or Medinan life by the Prophet Muhammad. He actually practiced monogamy with his wife Khadija for the bulk of his years. It was not until he was a widower in his fifties, and a new head of state in Medina, that Muhammad entered into the traditional practice. Over the final decade of his life and motivated by efforts to solidify political or tribal allegiances, he married some twelve women (accounts vary) in all, most of them widows. Two of the best known of Muhammad's wives during the Medinan period were Aisha bint Abu Bakr and Hafsa bint Umar, the daughters of caliphs who became Muhammad's two immediate political successors.

Tradition says that Aisha was just a girl at the time of her marriage to the Prophet Muhammad, a story that has been used to hurl abuses at Islam by its detractors, but among Muslims (Sunnis in particular) Lady Aisha is remembered for her knowledge and headstrong leadership. After the Prophet's death, she was acknowledged, even by the caliphs, as having special knowledge of Muhammad's ways, sayings, character, and practices (i.e., his sunna), and she handed down decisions and judgments on sacred laws and customs.[10] After unsuccessfully leading an army against the caliph Ali at the Battle of the Camel in 656, she retired to a quiet life of scholarship and religious instruction in Medina, teaching men and women alike.[11] She remains one of the most commonly cited early authorities for the transmission of the Hadith and interpretation of the Qur'an in Sunni Islam. For Sunni Muslims, she is among the best women to have ever lived.

Hafsa, the daughter of the caliph Umar, was a widow who married the Prophet Muhammad in early 625 after the Battle of Badr. She was well known for her devotion to prayer and fasting but best known for her knowledge of the Qur'an. Hafsa even committed the entirety of the sacred text to memory, and she was consulted for her knowledge of the Qur'an on many occasions. Greatly impressed by his daughter's knowledge, Caliph Umar entrusted into her care and protection upon his death the *suhuf* ("pages"), the earliest written documents of the Qur'an, as well as other matters of his inheritance. The suhuf of Hafsa later served as the basis for the canonical Qur'anic text established during the reign of the caliph Uthman—reportedly the Qur'an as we know it today. In addition Hafsa is credited alongside Aisha, Umm Habiba, Maymuna, and Umm Salama as a source of transmission for many prophetic traditions in the Hadith.

Due to the prominent role that women played in the transmission of prophetic traditions, especially the wives of the Prophet, the study of the Hadith has long been an intellectual arena of Islamic thought where Muslim women have prospered alongside male colleagues. In the generation after the companions (*sahaba*) of the Prophet, the notable female scholars of the Hadith included Umm al-Darda and Amra bint Abd al-Rahman. Recognized as the greatest scholar of the Hadith in her time by the respected *qadi* ("judge") of Basra, Ilyas ibn Muawiyya, Umm al-Darda's knowledge as a jurist and master of prophetic traditions reportedly rivaled that of famous scholars such as Hasan al-Basri. Meanwhile, Amra bint Abd al-Rahman was a teacher of the celebrated qadi of Medina, Abu Bakr ibn Hazm, who was ordered by the revered Caliph Umar ibn Abdel-Aziz to record all of the traditions transmitted on her authority. The next generation of Muslims produced yet more female scholars of the Hadith, including Abida al-Madaniyya, Abda bint Bashr, Umm Umar al-Thaqafiyya, Zaynab bint Sulayman, and Khadija umm Muhammad, among many others. Abida, in fact, was a former slave who studied the Hadith under scholars in Medina before traveling to Islamic Spain where she reportedly demonstrated mastery of some ten thousand traditions.[12] This legacy of learning continued into the ensuing centuries, among luminaries such as Fatima bint Abdel-Rahman, who was the granddaughter of Abu Dawud (compiler of the Sunan), Fatima bint al-Hasan ibn Ali al-Daqqaq, who was the wife of the mystic Abul-Qasim al-Qushayri, and Karima al-Marwaziyya, who was considered the preeminent authority on Sahih Bukhari in her time. Another twelfth century scholar, Shuhda, "the writer of Baghdad," is wonderfully described in classical biographies as "the calligrapher, the great authority of Hadith, and the pride of womanhood."[13]

In Egypt in the ninth century, one of the most beloved and renowned Muslim scholars was Lady Nafisa, a descendant of the Prophet Muhammad known affectionately as Nafisat al-'Ilm, meaning "gem of knowledge."[14] As a young woman in Medina, Nafisa studied under the revered jurist and scholar Malik ibn Anas, listening to his lectures in the front row and mastering his famous collection of Medinan prophetic traditions, al-Muwatta. Later in her life, many scholars traveled to study under Nafisa's tutelage, including the great jurists Ahmed ibn Hanbal and Imam Shafi'i.[15] In Egypt her friendship with Imam Shafi'i, the namesake of one of the four Sunni madhahib (schools of law), in particular has become a favorite source of legend and folk stories. One legend says that whenever Imam Shafi'i fell ill, he would send one of his students to Nafisa to ask her to pray for him, and by the time the student returned to Imam Shafi'i he would find the imam cured.[16] Today Nafisa's tomb in old Cairo is one of the most revered Islamic sites in the country, and she is considered one of the patron saints of the city.

Muslim women have not only been renowned scholars, but patrons of entire universities, such as the celebrated Qarawiyyin University in Fez. Founded in 859 as a mosque and madrassa, Qarawiyyin was established through an endowment from Fatima bint Muhammad al-Fihri, a wealthy migrant from Qayrawan (Kairouan), Tunisia.[17] She and her sister were well educated and inherited great wealth from their father, a successful businessman, which Fatima chose to devote to the establishment of a center of religious learning.[18] Elsewhere Rabia Khatun, the sister of the famous Saladin who liberated Jerusalem from the Crusaders, established a madrassa in Damascus (completed in 1245) known as al-Sahiba, for a Hanbali Syrian scholar whose daughter she had studied under for years.[19] A domed mausoleum in the madrassa also houses the tomb of Rabia, who died in 1246. Still other examples are the poetess Hajja Maryam bint Yaqub al-Ansari, who established a madrassa for girls in Seville in the eleventh century; Sayyida Hurra (Arwa al-Sulayhi), the Sulayhid queen (*malika*) of Yemen, who established numerous schools during her reign in the twelfth century; and Zahida Khatun, the queen of Fars, who founded a madrassa in the city of Shiraz in the twelfth century.[20]

The point of reviewing this material is not to overlook historical cases where Muslim women, especially among the lower classes, were excluded from an education or the misogynistic attitudes held by some male Muslim scholars, including some of the Prophet's own companions. Rather, this survey of the historical record shows that there is a clear precedent in Islamic history in support of the education and literacy of Muslim women, especially from the upper classes, dating back to the time of the Prophet Muhammad. Men, however, did outnumber women in the ranks of the scholars, and there were indeed opponents of women's education, but Islamic history suggests that such opposition was hardly ubiquitous and that many prominent scholars and rulers saw no conflict between Islam and women's education. Scholarly interaction between men and women, as well as the fact that women were taught by both women and men, is clearly documented.[21] A recent study of archival sources by Mohammad Akram Nadwi has identified eight thousand female scholars throughout Islamic history. The historical records are often scant regarding many of the details, but the existing evidence shows that women attended men's lectures (and vice versa) and men studied alongside women.[22] We should further note that the period traditionally recognized as the "golden age" of Islamic civilization was the same time when the education of women, especially among the middle and upper classes, was relatively common, and it is well documented. The decline of the great Islamic empires by the eighteenth century, however, meant a decline in opportunities, especially in the realm of knowledge, when the Muslim world lost its prior economic power and began to turn inward, losing pace in the advancement of knowledge and science to Europe.

Women and Nonviolence

Despite the fact that the five champions of nonviolence discussed in this book are men, the reader can be assured that this selection is not exhaustive. Notable female Muslim champions of nonviolence also exist, including Rebiya Kadeer and Iltezam Morrar (who is discussed in the next chapter). Known as the "Mother of Uighurs," Kadeer is the foremost challenger of the Chinese government's hardline rule over the Uighurs, an ethnically Turkic Muslim people in western China, whose homeland of Xinjiang (East Turkistan) was annexed by Communist China in 1949. "The [Chinese] government sees Islam as a threat," Kadeer has stated, "strictly restricting the practice of the religion in order to make our people faithless."[23] In 1999 Kadeer was arrested and tried in China, imprisoned for nearly six years, and, through diplomatic intervention, finally exiled to the United States.[24] Due to her struggle against the Chinese government, Kadeer has often been compared to the exiled Tibetan leader, the Dalai Lama. "Between the Uighurs and Tibetans, our suffering, our plight, is similar," Kadeer has said, "but after 9/11 the Chinese began to use propaganda against us [as Muslims] in a way that has intensified our problems."[25]

All five of the male scholars and leaders in this volume devoted considerable attention to the place of women in Muslim societies. Their views on the subject differ in some respects, but all of them have advocated for the education and advancement of Muslim women as a part of the "true Islam" that they envision. Badshah Khan was an outspoken advocate of women's rights and education throughout his life. Addressing a gathering of women in 1940 near Kohat, Pakistan, on the interrelated nature of his campaign for nonviolent resistance and the advancement of Pashtun women, he stated, "We are like the two wheels of a big chariot, and unless our movements have been mutually adjusted, our carriage will never move."[26] The martyr Mahmoud Taha evidently shared Badshah Khan's outspoken advocacy for women's rights and education. After all, he gave his life opposing the implementation of an archaic and discriminatory legal system ostensibly derived from Islam's sacred texts that would have imposed severe restrictions on women (both Muslim and non-Muslim) in Sudan. Furthermore, the activities carried out by Taha's many female Jumhuri followers in the public sphere, as discussed in chapter 6, were virtually unknown prior to that time and revolutionary in traditional Sudanese society.[27]

Maulana Wahiduddin Khan, like Badshah Khan and Taha, has demonstrated great concern for the status of women in Muslim societies. His chief spokesperson to the outside world, the chairperson of his Centre for Peace and Spirituality in New Delhi, is a female scholar, Dr. Farida Khanam. She is currently an associate professor in the Department of Islamic Studies at Jamia Millia Islamia (National Islamic University) in New Delhi. Khanam is the primary translator into English of Wahiduddin Khan's books and writings, including those cited in this book. Among his many writings, Wahiduddin Khan has devoted considerable attention to the education and status of women in modern Muslim societies. In one article devoted to the subject, he laments how far behind Muslim men and women have fallen in education. And he summons Muslims to recall a different age when things were very different. "There was a time," he writes, "when, during the Abbasid period, the highest point in Muslim culture, literacy was almost one hundred percent [and] not only men but all women received the education prevalent at that time." He argues that if Muslims would only "strive towards the goal of one hundred percent literacy," that feat alone would "suffice to bring about their overall reformation" and Muslims would emerge as a "developed community." Wahiduddin, in fact, puts women at the forefront of this campaign for education. He argues that "the literate woman's ability to read to her young children, and the example she sets in her own quest for knowledge are the most powerful stimuli in their educational progress."[28]

Meanwhile, the writings of the Syrian philosopher Jawdat Saeed stress the vital role that women must play in the struggle against violence throughout the world. In a statement by Saeed to a meeting in Kuala Lampur of the Muslim Women's Shura Council (an organization of prominent, educated, Muslim female leaders), he wrote that "female gentleness will overcome the harshness of men who so far have filled the earth with corruption and bloodshed" and "women will be able to usher in a new era of peace on earth which has been polluted with blood."[29] Clearly Saeed not only supports the education of women, but he imagines them at the forefront of the Islamic nonviolence movement.

Finally, Grand Ayatollah Muhammad al-Shirazi, while more conservative in his views than the other figures in this book, states in a treatise he wrote on the status of women within Twelver Shi'ite Islam that "the Islamic government, and before that the Islamic movement, must take a number of measures to address the honour and dignity of women as well as other aspects of her concern, [beginning by] arranging for the correct religious and modern education for girls."[30] Clearly, excluding women from education or basic literacy is not a part of the Islam envisioned or proposed by the ayatollah or any of the other Muslim champions of nonviolence.

Taking Action

The aforementioned 2005 UN report on education and gender equality has identified four points of action that regional and international organizations can use to improve the education of women in the developing world across religious or ethnic lines. These four points of action, as described in the report, are:

(1) Making girls' schooling more affordable by reducing fees and offering targeted scholarships.

(2) Building schools closer to girls' homes, involving the community in school management, and allowing flexible scheduling.

(3) Making schools girl-friendly by improving the safety of schools, the design of facilities, and instituting policies that promote girls' attendance.

(4) Improving the quality of education by training more female teachers for the secondary level, providing gender-sensitive textbooks, and developing a curriculum for girls that is strong in math and sciences and projects gender equality. [31]

Adopting the narrative of nonviolence is perfectly complimentary to all of these goals, and it can help to further facilitate all four points of action in modern Muslim societies, improving their success rates, financing, and geographic outreach.

Making education affordable is a formidable task that virtually all societies, including wealthy nations such as the United States, have found to be an ongoing challenge. The UN report on education and gender equality identifies two ways to make schooling more affordable for poor families in the developing world: eliminating fees and providing incentives for girls to attend.[32] For instance, the elimination of primary school fees in Tanzania in 2002 resulted in an additional enrollment of 1,500,000 students.[33] In Bangladesh, the homeland of microfinance pioneer Muhammad Yunus, a nationwide stipend program (ranging from twelve to thirty-six dollars per girl annually) initiated back in 1994 to improve girls' enrollment in secondary schools, including all madrassas, had a substantial impact on their enrollment, particularly in rural areas—surpassing that of boys.[34] The program provided funds for girls that covered tuition, exam costs, textbooks, uniforms, school supplies, and transportation.[35] According to the UN report, "in 2002, attendance was 91 percent for girls and 86 percent for boys, and 89 percent of girls obtained passing marks in year-end exams compared with 81 percent of boys."[36] To continue receiving their school stipends, the girls must maintain regular attendance, receive adequate marks, and remain unmarried. In Bangladesh, marriage is a significant reason for girls dropping out of school, particularly among poor, rural adolescents entering secondary education.[37] In these communities, marital considerations often serve as a basis for parental educational decisions for girls, rather than the potential for earnings in the labor markets.[38]

During the Innovative Financing for Education Conference held in New York City during the UN summit in September 2010, Queen Rania al-Abdullah of Jordan addressed a gathering of international leaders in politics and business on the need to develop innovative ways to fund education programs, such as the stipends for the girls of Bangladesh. "Funding everything from poverty reduction to childhood diseases and more, only through traditional aid avenues, is, well, overwhelming," Queen Rania stated, "and, let's be honest, not meeting expectations." The queen stressed that the billions of dollars in international aid currently designated for the UN Millennium Development Goals (MDGs) should be channeled to two MDGs in particular—namely, universal primary education, and gender equality and women's empowerment. These represent only two of the eight total MDGs. However, the queen noted, "they represent the whole," because "if every child around the world was in school and every woman and girl was educated and active in their communities, then these [two goals] could underpin success in all other development challenges."[39]

Decreasing the distance that students must travel to attend school is another vital challenge to overcome, especially for agrarian societies where rural communities remain far from the clusters of schools in the urban centers, such as Cairo or Kabul. This fact points not only to the need for the construction of new school facilities near those rural communities, it points to the need for adequate infrastructure (e.g., roads) and security to get students to the schools once they are built. In Egypt a recent campaign to construct rural primary schools resulted in the growth of girls' enrollment by 23 percent and boys' by 18 percent.[40] In the absence of local schools, families often send only their sons (if any children at all), who have to walk for hours along single-lane dirt roads to reach the nearest school.[41] In the small farming village of Abu Tig located in southern Egypt, far from the bustling cities of Cairo and Alexandria in the north, UNICEF supported the construction of a one-room schoolhouse in the village to provide access to girls, many of whom were the first females in their family to ever attend school or even learn how to read.[42]

The distances that students travel to reach their schools can often be dangerous, especially in destabilized states where violence remains endemic. Families are far more reluctant to send girls out into these environments, both out of concern for safety and notions of honor. Distance, however, is not the sole problem related to family concerns about safety. Some families have expressed apprehension over their girls' interaction with male teachers or peers, fearful of possible abuse or sexual misconduct. One technique proven to help allay these fears has been to hire female assistants to escort the girls or establish girls-only secondary schools.[43] Qualified female instructors and assistants are needed for such efforts, however, and they remain in short supply. Yet another issue that has deterred girls' attendance is the school facilities themselves, which may not meet the hygienic needs of female students. Private bathrooms, especially for postpubescent girls who may be menstruating, are essential.[44]

Finally, large rural families often depend on girls to care for their siblings and to complete daily chores, especially when poverty forces the parents to travel long distances to find work and to labor for long hours. Flexible school schedules and daycare centers, as well as incentives such as take-home rations, have all been shown to help alleviate these problems and motivate families to send their girls to school.[45] In studies of girls' education in parts of sub-Saharan Africa, it was found that girls, especially in rural communities, are overburdened with domestic responsibilities, including cooking for entire families (sometimes even for their schoolteachers), all forms of cleaning, and caring for younger siblings.[46] Despite the hardships and negative impact on the health and education of the girls, the families consider these practices necessary for their survival. As such, the factors at play go far beyond patriarchal or misogynistic attitudes toward girls' education in these societies.

Creating the Vanguard

Even in circumstances where female students have access to schools, the quality of the education must justify their enrollment and ongoing attendance. That means that there must be appropriate curriculums, study supplies (e.g., textbooks), and qualified instructors.[47] Regarding the last point, adult illiteracy remains a serious problem that can have serious cyclical effects. In addition, recent analyses of school textbooks in the Middle East, Asia, and Africa have consistently found stereotypical patriarchal material depicting women as subordinate and passive, and men as intelligent, dominant leaders.[48] Amending textbooks and course materials can provide institutions with an opportunity for intervention, and more suitable content and narratives (including those of figures such as Rebiya Kadeer) can play a transformative role in the lives of these students. Indeed, the incorporation into textbooks of Islamic nonviolence, as told through the narrative histories of the figures examined in this book, could place Muslim women at the vanguard of the nonviolence movement in the modern Muslim world, as Jawdat Saeed suggested. As with the other points of action listed here, these reforms all require significant financial investment and institutional support, which are conventionally depleted by military and security costs, including counterterrorism efforts to battle violent Islamist extremists.

The material I've examined in this chapter and the preceding ones must be understood as comprehensive and interrelated, providing a broad program for socioeconomic development in modern Muslim societies. Poverty is obviously a huge mitigating factor for access to education in a variety of ways. Microfinance institutions, as discussed in chapter 9, provide a pragmatic and proven method of alleviating poverty that allows the poor, through their own efforts (not via charity handouts), to integrate themselves into regional economies as independent and empowered agents. Violence, however, can profoundly disrupt these efforts in many ways, including the absorption of an inordinate amount of a country's economic resources, the disruption of trade channels, the destruction of infrastructure that takes years to build (perhaps even longer to replace), and the compromise of safety and security for adults and students alike. The sociopolitical grievances of any people, however, cannot simply be dismissed (nor is it the place of an outsider to dismiss them), especially in the face of ongoing injustice. The narrative of nonviolence, as we will examine in the concluding chapter, takes this important factor into consideration, while opening the door to new avenues for progress and prosperity that the perpetuation of violence can never achieve.

11

Jihad without Swords

"Jihad" is a term so maligned in the West that it seems simply beyond repair. Its mere mention conjures up images of terrible atrocities and terrorism. It slips from the lips of sneering conservative television and radio commentators warning America of its impending doom at the hands of the Muslim hordes. In large, ominous letters it is sprawled across the covers of countless books and protest placards offering the same dire warnings of the "Islamic threat" to the West. Meanwhile, Muslim extremists sing the praises of jihad as they cradle assault rifles and daggers in their arms or display explosive-laden vests across their chests. Yet the Qur'an, the sacred Word of Allah for Muslims, does summon believers to jihad, the struggle for righteousness: "Those who believe and fled into exile and struggle (*jahadu*) in the path of God with their wealth and their souls have the highest rank with God, and those are the ones who will triumph."[1] Jihad is essential to the believer. It represents action over passivity and determinism. The believers have a divine mandate to take responsibility for their plight and use their wealth and their very lives to bring about change in the world. The narrative of nonviolence is an expression of jihad—a jihad without swords.

Jihad as Activism

After his exile to Medina, the Prophet Muhammad is reported to have told his followers that "what is evil in a man is alarming laziness and unrestrained cowardice."[2] In case there is any question as to what the Prophet was referring to, Abu Dawud classified this saying in his famous collection of hadith under the section Kitab al-Jihad ("Book of Jihad"). The Prophet's statement makes very clear the connotation of jihad as activist in nature—boldness in action—where the believers are willing to exert themselves and sacrifice their comfort and blood for the cause of change. This is a required element of nonviolence, as the lives of Martin Luther King Jr., Mohandas Gandhi, and the Muslim figures discussed in this book can attest. Certainly Muslim jurists, particularly in the medieval age of expanding empires, took such traditions to support and encourage participation in military conquests. However, there is no question that the Hadith (let alone the Qur'an) also see jihad in much broader terms. For example, the following hadith from the most authoritative canonical collection, Sahih Bukhari, refers to jihad as service to one's parents:

> Narrated [by] Abdullah bin Amr: A man came to the Prophet asking his permission to take part in [military] jihad. The Prophet asked him, "Are your parents alive?" He replied in the affirmative. The Prophet said to him, "Then exert (jahadu) yourself in their service."[3]

Another hadith from Sahih Bukhari, related by Aisha, who was discussed in chapter 10 as a major transmitter of prophetic traditions, describes the hajj, the strenuous (historically deadly) pilgrimage to the holy city of Mecca, as jihad:

> Narrated [by] Aisha (mother of the faithful believers): I said, "O Allah's Apostle! Shouldn't we participate in holy battles and jihad along with you?" He replied, "The best and the most superior jihad is hajj which is accepted by Allah." Aisha added: Ever since I heard that from Allah's Apostle I have determined not to miss hajj.[4]

The concept of jihad is an expansive and powerful one, historically engrained in Islamic thought. Islam is often characterized as "a religion of orthopraxy," meaning that proper action, ritual, and practice are paramount. The demands of the sacred texts on the lives of believers are not easy and often require substantial effort. At a minimum, even when a believer's actions fall short, the proper intention (*niyya*) must exist. This is the domain of jihad: ongoing exerted effort to live a righteous life and change the conditions of society in beneficial ways.

Historically four categories have been used to organize the broad forms of jihad: jihad of the sword or hand, jihad of the tongue (e.g., speaking truth to a tyrant), jihad of the pen, and jihad of the heart or soul. But even those categories are too narrow or limited. Another famous hadith refers to two major categories of jihad: the lesser jihad (the military jihad) and the greater jihad (the jihad of the soul). It is worth noting that the juridical concept of ijtihad, or independent legal reasoning, has the same root as jihad (j-h-d), referring to an exertion of the intellect. Therefore, limiting such a rich concept as jihad to physical warfare—even a just war with numerous ethical qualifiers—is shockingly crude and befitting of the extremists who seek to shed innocent blood.

Martyrdom is obviously something deeply intertwined with jihad. Here again the concept of martyrdom in Islam is tremendously expansive and interrelated with the struggle to live a righteous life in a world of difficulties, tragedy, and uncertainty. According to the Hadith, the Prophet Muhammad reportedly spoke of martyrs (*shuhada*) not simply as those who died with righteous intent (niyya) on the battlefield, but those killed by a plague, by disease of the stomach, by drowning, by a collapsing building, by fire, during childbirth, while protecting personal property, by being thrown from a horse or camel, by the sting of a poisonous creature, or one who dies defending his or her family.[5] Tradition points to Sumayya bint Khayyat as the first martyr of Islam.[6] It is reported that she was tortured and stabbed to death after she refused to give up Islam and return to the worship of the pagan gods of Mecca. The Qur'an consoles such devoted believers by stating, "And if you are slain or die in the way of God, forgiveness and mercy from God are far better than all [the unbelievers] could amass."[7]

The texts and narratives about jihad that have been harnessed in the rhetoric of violent extremists and revolutionaries in the Muslim world can all be utilized and redirected in the cause of nonviolence, for the "struggle" might be one and the same, even though the methods are profoundly different. For example, an extremist may attack innocent Israeli civilians living in a settlement built in the occupied West Bank as a means to end the Israeli occupation and establish Palestinian independence. That struggle is essentially the same as that of Ayed Morrar, a nonviolent activist in the village of Budrus, although the means utilized by the two profoundly differ. Indeed, I have argued that the violence of the extremist is

pointless, doomed to failure, and abhorrently wasteful. It is only through reject-
ing the false promise of the narrative of violence that progress, prosperity, and
prestige can be attained.

Reform through Maslaha

It is important to turn now to the Islamic juridical concept of *maslaha*, which refers to the public interest. Modern Muslim grievances are real and cannot simply
be dismissed, especially if one considers that roughly one out of five people on
the planet is a Muslim. That does not mean, however, that the existing methods
used to address and resolve those grievances are always worthy of support or respect. Violence is abhorrent and befitting of a more primitive age. It must be condemned. In Islamic thought, these decisions are traditionally the responsibility of
legal scholars through juridical discourse. This is where the concept of maslaha
becomes important for our discussion of violence and nonviolence. Jihad may be
an obligation for Muslim believers, but violence is not.

Maslaha literally means a source or cause of well-being and good, but in
Islamic thought it refers to the intent or purpose of God's revealed law for humanity and human attainment of well-being in all mundane and otherworldly
affairs. Maslaha is one of the main procedural means to address legal change
in Islam, often used as a tool to determine laws when the sacred texts are silent
on a subject or an existing law requires reform due to the circumstances of the
time. As scholar Felicitas Meta Maria Opwis noted in her comprehensive study
of the historical development of maslaha, "the function of maslaha as a method
of law-finding and vehicle of legal change makes it an important legal principle,
especially in the contemporary period; today no book or pamphlet on Islamic law
is written without reference to it."[8]

The Egyptian reformist Shaykh Muhammad Abduh made extensive use of
maslaha when he set about "modernizing" sharia in nineteenth-century Egypt.
Trained in the hallowed halls of al-Azhar in Cairo, Abduh rebuked the religious
scholars of his time for their adherence to *taqlid* (imitation of the past), called for
the freedom to practice ijtihad, encouraged the articulation of a new *ijma* ("consensus") in keeping with modern circumstances, and, finally, the replacement of
the antiquated classical system of fiqh ("jurisprudence") with new laws formu-
lated through maslaha and following the dictates of reason (*'aql*).[9]

The concept of maslaha provides a well-established juridical basis for Muslim scholars to overturn the validity of violence as a means of jihad (or political and socioeconomic change) on the basis of the devastating effects (anathema to the common good) that it has had on the conditions and development of modern Muslim societies. There is likely no better evidence to support this notion than the war-torn land of Afghanistan. Three decades of war, enacted by factions attempting to bring about desired change and prosperity (albeit sometimes along ethnic lines), have yielded nothing but rubble, ashes, and the most alarming humanitarian conditions one can imagine. For instance, the 2007–2008 National Risk and Vulnerability Assessment found that 7.4 million people (a third of the population) are unable to get enough food to live active, healthy lives, and another 8.5 million people, or 37 percent, are on the borderline of food insecurity. Afghanistan, as described in chapter 2, suffers from one of the highest levels of infant mortality and maternal mortality in the world.[10] The U.S. government estimates that there are 153 infant deaths for every one thousand live births in Afghanistan, giving it the second-highest infant mortality rate in the world after only Angola. The levels of violence and its broader repercussions have been so harmful that the continuation of life itself seems at risk. It is simply imperative that the false promises of the narrative of violence are exposed through all means and conveyed to the people that it afflicts the worst (if they still cling to it).

On the Ground

Offering an alternative narrative, such as articulating a persuasive argument for Islamic nonviolence through the teachings and extraordinary lives of the Muslim scholars, leaders, and activists discussed in this book, is a starting point. So too is building skill sets for nonviolence, such as those explored by American academic Gene Sharp (*From Dictatorship to Democracy*) and Palestinian American scholar Mohammed Abu-Nimer.

The director of the Conflict Resolution Skills Institute in Washington, D.C., Abu-Nimer has focused on the practical applications of nonviolence initiatives, such as the practice of *sulha* (arbitration) in the Arab world. Devoted exclusively to the Arab-Muslim context, Abu-Nimer's study "seeks to actively promote peace-building and nonviolence strategies and values rooted in the indigenous Islamic cultural and religious contexts, focusing on the identification of Islamic values, rituals, stories, and worldviews."[11] In his review of the nonviolent methods used during the First Intifada in 1987, Abu-Nimer identifies the value of economic noncooperation, social noncooperation, protest and persuasion, political nonco-operation, and symbolic expression. The physical and symbolic focal points of the nonviolent resistance were the mosques, serving as organizing and teaching centers.[12] Demonstrations and marches often began at them, especially after Friday congregational prayers, and the buildings themselves became canvases for symbolic resistance with the walls and minarets being covered with posters and paintings of the Palestinian national flag or slogans of the resistance.[13]

Grievances such as the occupation of Muslim lands by foreign powers or the tyranny of an authoritarian government must be met with aggressive campaigns of nonviolent resistance. Muslim women in particular may serve as the vanguard for this struggle. The narrative of nonviolence, articulated in chapter 3, related that when the means used by the power structure to maintain its dominance are exposed as unjustified, the subsequent loss of prestige causes the power structure to falter and the conditions of the community are reformed justly, according to the popular will and means of the community. Therefore, attempts to crack down on women, especially if visually documented for the world to witness, would undoubtedly prove effective at exposing the unjustified brutality of the power structure. Many societies throughout the world regard attacks against unarmed women as beyond all acceptable boundaries. Although there are exceptions, Muslim jurists have historically argued that women should be excluded from participating in warfare, meaning combat. In the case of nonviolent resistance, it would seem that this traditional restriction would no longer apply. Thus an army of women could act as a vanguard and confront an armed force of the power structure nonviolently, with a potentially tremendous effect. A documentary film directed by Julia Bacha has documented one inspiring example of such resistance in the West Bank.

In 2002 the Israel Defense Forces (IDF) began plans to expand the well-known Israeli security wall through the Palestinian village of Budrus, the completion of which would have divided the residents of the farming village from their source of livelihood, their historic olive groves and effectively imprisoned them in an enclave. "The 1,200 residents of Budrus—the vast majority of whom depend on agriculture for work—will lose a large portion of their fields," *The Nation* reported. "An Israeli bulldozer has already carved a preliminary path, and uprooted trees lie in its wake."[14] Led by activist Ayed Morrar, the residents of Budrus organized a campaign of nonviolence against the IDF, and it was the women who emerged on the frontlines. Led by Morrar's teenage daughter Iltezam Morrar, who once blocked an Israeli bulldozer by diving in front of it, the women of Budrus persevered, even as they were beaten, tear-gassed, and shot with rubber bullets. Israel finally rerouted the barrier wall to bypass nearly all of the village.[15]

Badshah Khan called nonviolent resistance such as that employed in Budrus "the weapon of the Prophet." His army of nonviolent soldiers, the Khudai Khidmatgars, utilized a range of tactics in their historic struggle against the British Empire. These tactics included forming human roadblocks; conducting hunger strikes, speech rallies, protests, and marches; boycotting British products; refusing to cooperate with, and resigning from, all state institutions; establishing independent Pashtun-language schools; producing illegal publications; using symbolic imagery, such as red uniforms; and undertaking acts of sabotage, followed by voluntary confessions.

The Qissa Khawani Bazaar massacre, discussed in chapter 4, was perhaps the most heroic and tragic act of the Khudai Khidmatgars' nonviolent resistance. Their disciplined sacrifice on that terrible day ultimately strengthened the independence movement and helped bring an end to British rule in India by exposing the unjustifiable means employed by those in power to maintain their dominance. But that awful massacre was more than eighty years ago, long before the age of modern media. The recent impact of new media on nonviolent resistance has been profound, as recent events in Egypt and Tunisia have demonstrated. If the killing of the Khudai Khidmatgars had occurred in the past several years, video footage of the atrocity would have traveled around the world on the Internet and cable news outlets in a matter of minutes. The international outcry would have been deafening. Even before the age of new media, the brutality inflicted on civil rights activists in the American South, such as during the march in 1963 from Selma to Montgomery, when fire hoses, police batons, and dogs were used against unarmed men and women, horrified the nation and the rest of the world watching on television. The role of the media was instrumental to the success of the Civil Rights movement, and that was before the power of communication was put into the hands of the common people via websites such as YouTube and technology such as cell-phone cameras.

The case of Neda Agha-Soltan, a twenty-six-year-old Iranian woman killed during the 2009 postelection protests in Tehran, provides a vivid, yet tragic, example of the power of new media. As she stood beside her music teacher on a quiet street near the site of ongoing protests against the fraudulent reelection of hardliner Mahmoud Ahmedinejad, Agha-Soltan was shot in the chest by a sniper's bullet. She fell quickly to the ground, blood spilled from her chest, nose, and mouth, and she died there on the street in the arms of her teacher and an off-duty doctor trying desperately to revive her. The entire horrific scene was caught on video with a cell phone and transmitted around the world within hours, quickly appearing on YouTube and elsewhere. That day, Neda Agha-Soltan became a media phenomenon, and her image was printed on placards and brandished at demonstrations around the world.[16] Despite her general disinterest in politics, she became the hero of the popular resistance against the authoritarian Iranian regime. She was now the unwilling champion and symbol of nonviolent resistance against the Iranian power structure. Her death provoked outrage in Iran and abroad, particularly among women, who have been at the forefront of the protest movement in Iran.[17] Fearful of the power that Agha-Soltan's death could have against their regime, Iran's government used paramilitary forces to break up public attempts to mourn her and ordered her body buried immediately without a memorial service.[18] Her grave has since been repeatedly desecrated by supporters of the regime, her family monitored by state operatives, and three documentaries broadcast by state-run television have tried to discredit the events surrounding her death. "They have broadcast three films and each time contradicted their earlier claims," her mother has said.[19] Clearly the short, grainy cell-phone video of Neda Agha-Soltan's tragic death, taken by an amateur on the streets of Tehran, has proven to be among the most formidable weapons against the Iranian regime, although the difficult struggle continues.

In Egypt the young revolutionaries of the "Arab Spring" that toppled the authoritarian regime of Hosni Mubarak in 2011 utilized new media with tremendous success, largely within a secular nonviolent framework. Indeed, it is particularly noteworthy that one of the most prominent faces of the Egyptian revolution was an executive from Internet powerhouse Google, Wael Ghonim. It was Ghonim who established the popular Facebook page "We are all Khaled Saeed," which served as a rallying point for the uprising. Khaled Saeed was a twenty-eight-year-old Internet user in Alexandria who was dragged from an Internet café by Egyptian police and beaten to death on June 6, 2010. Disturbing photographs of Saeed's mutilated corpse later went viral online and sparked a wave of outrage that helped mobilize the January 25, 2011, protests on "National Police Day" in Egypt. Throughout the revolution, YouTube, Twitter, Facebook, and satellite television all proved instrumental in subverting the regime's media propaganda apparatus. In the United States, ABC News described the horrific image of Saeed's broken face as "the face that launched a revolution."[20]

Toward a Mass Movement

The question that must now be asked is, how can the teachings and narratives of Islamic nonviolence go from lectures, books, and new media into a large-scale and sustained Muslim social movement for change? The spread of violent extremist ideology across the globe has been accomplished largely through new media by individuals and groups articulating a dominant (albeit fragmented and flawed) narrative linking Islam to unrestrained violence under the guise of jihad.[21] The narrative of violence is produced and reproduced in everyday talk and mediated forums. As a result, any hope of informed and civil public discourse about the relationships among Islam, Muslim communities, and the West has been effectively "hijacked" by those who promote the enactment of the binary narrative of violence (including public figures and members of our own governments). The narrative of violence is reified through such communication, particularly in the context of an increasingly global network and mediated environment. The formation of a large-scale social movement thus requires the creation of discursive space for alternative narratives that disrupt and potentially transform the dominant narrative framework using a multidimensional approach.

The often marginalized voices of Islamic nonviolence must be amplified. This effort will require sustained scholarly and public engagement, including workshops, conferences, publications, and media products. The Muslim champions of nonviolence included in this book were selected for a specific set of criteria. Despite the common erroneous assumption that "Muslim" and "Arab" are virtually synonymous, Islam is a truly global religion, and 80 percent of the world's 1.57 billion Muslims are non-Arabs. The full diversity of the Muslim world requires attention. The figures chosen modestly represent this variety and the range of cultures in the Muslim world. The five figures also represent significant voices from both the Sunni and Shi'ite branches of Islam with elements of Sufism included. Thus these figures can be utilized differently in specific regions where the narratives will resonate with communities the strongest. The transformation of their teachings and narratives into new media products utilizing advanced information and social networking technologies, such as cell phones, has a great deal of potential. Extremists, meanwhile, continue to demonstrate the effectiveness of new media (e.g., al-Qaeda's As-Sahab Foundation for Islamic Media Publication) as an outlet for the dissemination of their interpretation of Islam and ideological message. So too must proponents of nonviolence.

In recent years Western governments and analysts have spoken about the need to identify and engage "moderate" Muslims overseas. However, it remains unclear what the West means by "moderate." If Western governments and analysts mean secular, passively pro-American, and subservient to American interests, then the Muslim champions of nonviolence examined in this book do not fall under the category of Muslim "moderates." If, however, a "moderate" Muslim is someone who does not resort to terrorism or violence, and does not persecute ethnic and religious minorities, as a means to resolve their grievances (many of which may be legitimate and against America and its allies), then these are certainly the "moderates" that they seek. Westerners, who are often designated as the Other in the narrative of violence, must better articulate whom they hope to engage and form partnerships with inside the Muslim world. At present it seems that the parameters are too restrictive and unrealistic. If, for instance, there is anti-American sentiment among non-Muslim societies in France or Venezuela, then why should we expect differently of peoples in predominantly Muslim societies?

In 1961 Martin Luther King Jr. stated, "[Today] the choice is no longer between violence and nonviolence; it is either nonviolence or nonexistence."[22] The growing number of countries that have nuclear ambitions should make us all heed his warning more than ever. Led by Iran, a growing number of Muslim states are now pondering pursuit of nuclear arms and joining the Muslim state of Pakistan. Dismayed by such developments and the ongoing violence in the world, a growing number of international commentators have recently asked, where is the King or Gandhi of Islam? For instance, *New York Times* columnist Nicholas Kristof wrote an op-ed in July 2010 titled "Waiting for Gandhi," addressing the need to develop nonviolent resistance strategies among Muslim Palestinians in the West Bank. Similarly a documentary film about nonviolent strategies in the Palestinian territories, the aforementioned *Budrus*, premiered at international film festivals and received growing attention. In addition, the conservative *Weekly Standard* published an article in April 2009 by Gershon Gorenberg titled "The Missing Mahatma: Searching for a Gandhi or a Martin Luther King in the West Bank," which fantasized about the possibility of a nonviolent Islamic social movement developing out of the teachings of Jawdat Saeed. And in 2008 the *Los Angeles Times* carried a story about Canadian filmmaker Teri McLuhan and her documentary on "The Frontier Gandhi" of Pakistan, Abdul Ghaffar "Badshah" Khan. It seems clear that at a time when violent images of the Muslim world dominate our headlines, people around the world are increasingly interested in the champions of Islamic nonviolence—the jihad without swords—and what it could mean for our shared planet. Perhaps this book has helped the reader to better understand Islamic nonviolence and its basis in Islam's rich sacred texts. It is my ultimate hope that those searching for a Muslim King will find him.

NOTES

Chapter 1: Jihad and the Book

1. Ali ibn Abu Talib, "Sermon 124," in *Nahjul Balagha: Peak of Eloquence*, ed. Yasine T. al-Jabouri (Elmhurst, NY: Tahrike Tarsile Qur'an Inc., 1996), 278.
2. Kevin Rushby, *Children of Kali: Through India in Search of Bandits, the Thug Cult, and the British Raj* (New York: Walker, 2002).
3. Jeffry R. Halverson, *Theology and Creed in Sunni Islam: The Muslim Brotherhood, Ash'arism, and Political Sunnism* (New York: Palgrave Macmillan, 2010), 61.
4. Herfried Münkler, *Empires: The Logic of World Domination from Ancient Rome to the United States*, trans. Patrick Camiller (Malden, MA: Polity Press, 2007), 5.
5. David Nicolle and Graham Turner, *Poitiers AD 732: Charles Martel Turns the Islamic Tide* (New York: Osprey, 2008), 29.
6. Renée Hirschon, ed., *Crossing the Aegean: An Appraisal of the 1923 Compulsory Population Exchange between Greece and Turkey* (New York: Berghahn Books, 2003).
7. Anthony Aust, *Handbook of International Law*, 2nd ed. (New York: Cambridge University Press, 2010), 36.

Chapter 2: False Promise

1. Hans Magnus Enzensberger, *Civil Wars: From L.A. to Bosnia* (New York: New Press, 1993), 11.
2. Phillip L. Walker, "A Bioarcheological Perspective on the History of Violence," *Annual Review of Anthropology* 30 (2001): 573.
3. See, e.g., Jonathan Gottschall and David Sloan Wilson, eds., *The Literary Animal: Evolution and the Nature of Narrative* (Chicago: Northwestern University Press, 2005); Jeffry R. Halverson, H. L. Goodall Jr., and Steven R. Corman, *Master Narratives of Islamist Extremism* (New York: Palgrave Macmillan, 2011).
4. Christian Mesquida and Neil Werner, discussion summary, "Young Men and War: Could We Have Predicted the Distribution of Violent Conflicts at the End of the Millennium?" Woodrow Wilson International Center for Scholars website (June 22, 2001), http://www.wilsoncenter.org/index.cfm?fuseaction=events.event_summary&event_id=7094.

5. Quoted in Michael White, *Isaac Asimov: A Life of the Grand Master of Science Fiction* (New York: Carroll & Graf Publishers, 1994), 72.
6. Quoted in *The Suez Canal Problem, 26 July–22 September 1956,* U.S. Department of State Publication No. 6392 (Washington, DC: Government Printing Office, 1956), 345–51, available at the Fordham University website, http://www.fordham.edu/halsall/mod/1956Nasser-suez1.html.
7. Andrew Hammond, *Popular Culture in the Arab World: Arts, Politics, and Media* (New York: American University in Cairo Press, 2007), 20.
8. Quoted in Montasser al-Zayyat, *The Road to al-Qaeda: The Story of Bin Laden's Right Hand Man*, trans. Ahmed Fekhry (London: Pluto, 2004), 23.
9. Noam Chomsky, *9-11* (New York: Seven Stories, 2001), 20.
10. Abdullah Azzam, *Join the Caravan, the Second Edition* (1988), 6.
11. Ibid., 3.
12. Seth G. Jones, *Counterinsurgency in Afghanistan* (Washington, DC: Rand Corporation, 2008), 27.
13. Ibid.
14. "In-Depth: Laying Landmines to Rest? Humanitarian Mine Action," *IRIN News* (May 11, 2010), http://www.irinnews.org/InDepthMain.aspx?InDepthId=19&ReportId=62811&Country=Yes.
15. Mine Action Coordination Centre for Afghanistan, *Mine Action Strategic Guideline 2008–2013* (2009), 5.
16. "Corruption Contributes to Poverty in Afghanistan—UN," BBC News (March 30, 2010), http://news.bbc.co.uk/2/hi/8595258.stm.
17. *CIA World Fact Book 2011*, Central Intelligence Agency, https://www.cia.gov/library/publications/the-world-factbook/geos/eg.html.
18. UNICEF, http://www.unicef.org/egypt/overview.html.
19. Fareed Zakaria, "Pakistan Is 'Epicenter of Islamic Terrorism,'" CNN (May 5, 2010), http://ac360.blogs.cnn.com/2010/05/05/pakistan-is-epicenter-of-islamic-terrorism/?iref=allsearch.
20. *CIA Fact Book.*
21. Ibid.
22. Nicholas D. Kristof, "Pakistan and Times Square," *New York Times* (May 12, 2010), http://www.nytimes.com/2010/05/13/opinion/13kristof.html?hp.
23. Rod Nordland, "Disaster in Somalia," *Newsweek* (May 18, 2007), http://www.newsweek.com/id/34629.
24. "Somalia," World Vision UK, http://www.worldvision.org.uk/server.php?show=nav.1935.
25. Bruce Lincoln, *Holy Terrors: Thinking about Religion after September 11* (Chicago: University of Chicago Press, 2005), 6.
26. Jose Casanova, *Public Religions in the Modern World* (Chicago: University of Chicago Press, 1994).
27. Leonard Binder, *Islamic Liberalism: A Critique of Development Ideologies* (Chicago: University of Chicago Press, 1988).
28. Sayyid Qutb, *Milestones* (USA: SIME Journal, 2005), 38.
29. Osama bin Laden statement of March 19, 2009, translated by Open Source Center, https://www.opensource.gov/portal/server.pt/gateway/PTARGS_0_0_916

_314_0_43/http;/apps.opensource.gov;7011/opensource.gov/content/Display
/FEATURE/FEA20090319833838?action=advancedSearch.

30. Philip Johnston, "July 7 Preacher Abdullah El-Faisal Deported," *The Telegraph* (May 25, 2007), http://www.telegraph.co.uk/news/uknews/1552580/July-7 -preacher-Abdullah-El-Faisal-deported.html.

31. "Hate Preaching Cleric Jailed," BBC News (March 7, 2003), http://news.bbc.co .uk/2/ hi/uk_news /england/2829059.stm.

32. Bill Nichols, "Video Shows Beheading of American Captive," *USA Today* (May 11, 2004), http://www.usatoday.com/news/world/iraq/2004-05-11-iraq-beheading _x.htm.

33. "Radicals vs. Moderates: British Muslims at Crossroads," CNN (January 22, 2007), http://www.cnn.com/2007/WORLD/europe/01/17/warwithin.overview/.

34. Martha Stout, *The Sociopath Next Door* (New York: Broadway, 2005), 5.

35. Bin Laden statement of March 19, 2009.

36. Ibid.

37. Hannah Arendt, *On Violence* (New York: Harcourt, Brace & World, 1970), 5.

Chapter 3: Nonviolence

1. Daniel M. Mayton II, *Nonviolence and Peace Psychology: Intrapersonal, Interpersonal, Societal, and World Peace* (New York: Springer, 2009), vi.

2. Elihu Burritt and Charles Northend, *Elihu Burritt: A Memorial Volume Containing a Sketch of His Life and Labors* (New York: D. Appleton, 1880), 24.

3. Alexander Tyrrell, "Making the Millennium: The Mid-Nineteenth Century Peace Movement," *The Historical Journal* 21, no. 1 (March, 1978): 86.

4. Burritt and Northend, *Elihu Burritt*, 28.

5. Tyrrell, "Making the Millennium," 86, 87.

6. Tom H. Hastings, *The Lessons of Nonviolence: Theory and Practice in a World of Conflict* (Jefferson, NC: McFarland, 2006), 64.

7. Leo Tolstoy, *The Kingdom of God Is within You*, trans. Constance Garnett (New York: Kessinger, 2004), 5.

8. "Leo Tolstoy," *Encyclopedia Britannica* (accessed April 6, 2012), http://search .eb.com.ezproxy1.lib.asu.edu/eb/article-13425.

9. Ibid.

10. Martin Green, "Tolstoy as Believer," *Wilson Quarterly* 5, no. 2 (Spring 1981): 171–72. See also J. H. Abraham, "The Religious Ideas and Social Philosophy of Tolstoy," *International Journal of Ethics* 40, no. 1 (October 1929): 105–120.

11. Green, "Tolstoy as Believer," 171.

12. Leo Tolstoy, "The Root of the Evil," *North American Review* 172, no. 533 (April 1901): 493.

13. Michael A. Denner, "Tolstoy, Leo Nikolayevich," ed. James R. Millar, *Encyclopedia of Russian History*, vol. 4 (New York: Macmillan Reference USA, 2004), 1560.

14. Leo Tolstoy, *Writings on Civil Disobedience and Nonviolence* (Philadelphia, PA: New Society Publishers, 1987), 250.

15. Mohandas K. Gandhi, "Introduction," *A Letter to a Hindu: The Subjection of India, Its Cause and Cure* (1909), Anarchy Archives, http://dwardmac.pitzer.edu /Anarchist_Archives/bright/tolstoy/lettertodh indu.html.

16. Stanley Wolpert, "Gandhi, Mahatma M. K.," in *Encyclopedia of India*, vol. 2, ed. Stanley Wolpert (Detroit: Charles Scribner's Sons, 2006), 121.
17. Manfred B. Steger, *Judging Nonviolence: The Dispute between Realists and Idealists* (New York: Routledge, 2003), 62.
18. Quoted in John Dear, "The Experiments of Gandhi: Nonviolence in the Nuclear Age," *Peace Is the Way: Writings on Nonviolence from the Fellowship of Reconciliation*, ed. Walter Wink (New York: Orbis Books, 2000), 113.
19. Kathryn Tidrick, *Gandhi: A Political and Spiritual Life* (London: I. B. Tauris, 2006), 152.
20. Wolpert, "Gandhi, Mahatma M. K.," 122.
21. Ibid., 124.
22. Martin Luther King Jr., *The Autobiography of Martin Luther King Jr.*, ed. Clayborne Carson (New York: Grand Central, 2001), 23.
23. Ibid., 23–24.
24. Ibid., 24.
25. Ibid., 26.
26. Steger, *Judging Nonviolence*, 78–79.
27. Ibid., 79.
28. King, *Autobiography*, 137.
29. Martin Luther King Jr., "Letter from a Birmingham Jail" (April 1963), African Studies Center, University of Pennsylvania http://www.africa.upenn.edu/Articles_Gen/Letter_Birmingham.html.
30. Martin Luther King Jr., "Acceptance Speech" (December 16, 1964), Nobel Prize, http://nobelprize.org/nobel_prizes/peace/laureates/1964/king-acceptance.html.
31. Martin Luther King Jr., "Why We Can't Wait," in *A Testament of Hope: The Essential Writings and Speeches of Martin Luther King Jr.*, ed. James Melvin Washington (New York: HarperCollins, 1986), 524.
32. Manfred Berg, "King, Martin Luther, Jr.," in *Encyclopedia of African American History 1896 to the Present*, ed. Paul Finkelman (New York: Oxford University Press, 2009), http://www.oxford-africanamericanhistory2.com/entry?entry=t0005.e0693.
33. Ibid.
34. Martin Luther King Jr., "A Time to Break Silence," in *Testament of Hope*, ed. Washington, 234.
35. Berg, "King, Martin Luther, Jr."
36. David J. Garrow, *Bearing the Cross: Martin Luther King Jr. and the Southern Christian Leadership Conference* (New York: HarperCollins, 1986), 595–96.
37. Ibid., 597.
38. Jeff Cohen and Norman Solomon, "The Martin Luther King You Don't See on TV," FAIR (January 4, 1995), http://www.fair.org/index.php?page=2269.
39. Jim Forest, "People Are Willing to Sacrifice Themselves," in *Peace Is the Way*, ed. Wink, 227.
40. Quoted in Forest, "People Willing Sacrifice Themselves," 229.
41. Utah Phillips and Ani DiFranco, "Natural Resources," *The Past Didn't Go Anywhere*, recorded 1996, Righteous Babe Records, compact disc.
42. Desmond Tutu, "Nobel Lecture" (December 11, 1984), Nobel Prize, http://nobelprize.org/nobel_prizes/peace/laureates/1984/tutu-lecture.html.

43. Quoted in Matthew Duss, "A History of Nonviolence," *The American Prospect* (November 15, 2007), http://www.prospect.org/cs/articles?article=a_history_of_nonviolence.

44. Quoted in Robert Cohen and Reginald E. Zelnik, eds., *The Free Speech Movement: Reflections on Berkeley in the 1960s* (Berkeley: University of California Press, 2002), 119.

45. Elizabeth Janeway, "On the Power of the Weak," *Signs* 1, no. 1 (Autumn 1975): 105.

46. Hastings, *Lessons of Nonviolence*, 32.

47. "A Short History of Grameen Bank," Grameen Bank, http://www.grameen-info.org/index.php?option=com_content&task=view&id=19&Itemid=114.

48. The Norwegian Nobel Committee, "Press Release: The Nobel Peace Prize for 2006" (Oslo: October 16, 2006), Nobel Prize, http://nobelprize.org/nobel_prizes/peace/laureates/2006/press.html.

49. "Frequently Asked Questions," FINCA, http://www.finca.org/site/c.erKPI2PCIo E/b. 2394157/k.8161/Frequently_Asked_Questions.htm.

50. "Narrative History," FINCA, http://www.finca.org/site/c.erKPI2PCIoE/b.2604291 /k. 9ADF/Narrative_History.htm.

51. David Belgum, "Re-Exploring Anger: Its Dynamics and Treatment," *Journal of Religion and Health* 26, no. 4 (Winter 1987), 280.

52. Stuart Fox, "Laws Might Change as the Science of Violence Is Explained," Live Science (June 7, 2010), http://www.livescience.com/culture/Laws-Might-Change -as-the-Science-of-Violence-Is-Explained-100607.html.

53. Jeanna Bryner, "Humans Crave Violence Just Like Sex," LiveScience (January 17, 2008), http://www.livescience.com/health/080117-violent-cravings.html.

54. Arendt, *On Violence*, 53.

Chapter 4: The Chieftain

1. Aisha Ahmad and Roger Boase, *Pashtun Tales from the Pakistan-Afghan Frontier* (London: Saqi Books, 2003), 13.

2. Abdul Ghaffar Khan (Badshah Khan), *My Life and Struggle*, trans. Helen H. Bouman (Delhi: Hind Pocket Books, 1969), 9.

3. Quoted in Eknath Easwaran, *A Man to Match Mountains: Badshah Khan, Nonviolent Soldier of Islam* (Berkeley: Nilgiri, 1984), 40–41.

4. Khan, *My Life and Struggle,* 11.

5. Ibid.

6. Ibid., 12–13.

7. Ibid., 13–14.

8. Ibid., 24.

9. Ibid.

10. Ibid.

11. Ibid., 28–29.

12. Ibid., 20.

13. Ibid.

14. Ibid., 21.

15. Ibid., 23.

16. Ibid., 26.

17. Ibid.
18. Ibid., 29.
19. Sana Haroon, *Frontier of Faith: Islam in the Indo-Afghan Borderland* (New York: Columbia University Press, 2007), 93.
20. Lion M. G. Agrawal, *Freedom Fighters of India* (New Delhi, India: Isha Books, 2008), 124.
21. Easwaran, *Man to Match Mountains*, 79.
22. Ibid., 77.
23. Khan, *My Life and Struggle*, 40.
24. Ibid., 41.
25. Ibid., 52.
26. Ibid., 55.
27. Ibid., 58.
28. Ian Talbot, *Pakistan: A Modern History* (New York: Palgrave Macmillan, 1999), 389.
29. Gail Minault, *The Khilafat Movement: Religious Symbolism and Political Mobilization in India* (New York: Columbia University Press, 1982), 169.
30. Khan, *My Life and Struggle*, 85.
31. Ibid., 86.
32. Ibid.
33. Easwaran, *Man to Match Mountains*, 104.
34. Khan, *My Life and Struggle*, 88.
35. Ibid., 90.
36. Ibid., 92.
37. Ibid., 97.
38. Ibid.
39. Ibid., 101.
40. "Saying of Baacha Khan," Baacha Khan Trust Educational Foundation (June 11, 2009), http://www.bkefoundation.org/index.php/about-us/saying-of-baacha-khan.
41. Quoted in Easwaran, *Man to Match Mountains*, 117.
42. Qur'an 42:40–43, translated by Abdullah Yusuf Ali.
43. Qur'an 41:34, translated by Abdullah Yusuf Ali.
44. Khan, *My Life and Struggle,* 103. See also Om Gupta, "Qissa Khwani Bazaar Massacre," in *The Encyclopedia of India, Pakistan, and Bangladesh* (Isha Books, 2006), 1969.
45. Eswaran, *Man to Match Mountains*, 122–23.
46. Ibid.
47. Vaqas Asghar, "Qissa Khawani Bazaar Massacre: Standing Tall before a Hail of Gunfire," *The Express Tribune*, April 24, 2011, http://tribune.com.pk/story/155404 /qissa-khawani-bazaar-massacre-standing-tall-before-a-hail-of-gunfire.
48. Khan, *My Life and Struggle*, 104.
49. Quoted in Eknath Easwaran, *Nonviolent Soldier of Islam* (Tomales, CA: Nilgiri, 2002), 125.
50. Khan, *My Life and Struggle*, 111.
51. Quoted in Easwaran, *Man to Match Mountains*, 141.
52. Khan, *My Life and Struggle*, 143.
53. Ibid., 145.
54. Ibid., 157.

55. Ibid., 160–61.
56. Ibid., 175.
57. Ibid., 182.
58. Ibid., 197.
59. Ibid., 207.
60. Ibid.
61. Easwaran, *Nonviolent Soldier of Islam*, 226.
62. Ibid., 233.
63. Talbot, "Abdul Ghaffar Khan," 391.

Chapter 5: The Philosopher

1. Jawdat Saeed, "Jawdat Saeed Answers Twelve Questions Posed," *Current Islamic Issues* (April 1998), http://www.jawdatsaid.net/en/index.php?title=Interview_with_Current_Islamic_Issues.
2. "Malek Bennabi," Philosophers of the Arabs (2010), http://www.arabphilosophers.com/ English/philosophers/modern/modern-names/eMalek_Ben_nabi.htm.
3. Quoted in Saeed, "Jawdat Saeed Answers."
4. See Muhammad Iqbal, *The Reconstruction of Islamic Thought* (Gloucestershire, UK: Dodo, 2009).
5. Saeed, "Jawdat Saeed Answers."
6. Azzam S. Tamimi, *Rachid Ghannouchi: A Democrat within Islamism* (New York: Oxford, 2001), 22.
7. Qur'an 5:27–30, trans. by Yusuf Ali and edited by Halverson.
8. Qur'an 2:30, trans. by Yusuf Ali and edited by Halverson.
9. Jawdat Saeed, *The Doctrine of Adam's First Son*, trans. Munzer A. Absi and H. Hilwani (Damascus: Dar al-Fikr, 1993), 69.
10. Ibid., 71.
11. Ibid., 51.
12. Ibid., 69.
13. Ibid., 19.
14. Ibid., 29.
15. Ibid., 34.
16. Ibid., 43.
17. Ibid., 19.
18. Ibid., 40.
19. Qur'an 2:256, translated by Halverson.
20. Saeed, "Jawdat Saeed Answers."
21. Saeed, *Doctrine of Adam's First Son*, 42.
22. Saeed, "Jawdat Saeed Answers."
23. Qur'an 16:125, translated by Halverson.
24. Saeed, "Jawdat Saeed Answers."
25. Ibid.; Qur'an 13:17.
26. Saeed, "Jawdat Saeed Answers."
27. Ibid.
28. Saeed, *Doctrine of Adam's First Son*, 47.
29. Ibid.

30. Ibid., 52.
31. Ibid., 53.
32. Malik Bennabi, foreword to Jawdat Saeed, *Hatta Yughayyiru Ma Bi-Anfusihim* (Damascus, 1972), retrieved from Jawdat Said, http://www.jawdatsaid.net, translated by Halverson.
33. Jawdat Saeed, "Madakhil Kitab Hatta Yughayyiru," in ibid.
34. Saeed, "Jawdat Saeed Answers."
35. Saeed, *Hatta Yughayyiru Ma Bi-Anfusihim*, 13.
36. Jawdat Saeed, "Muqaddimah Kitab Iqra wa Rabukal Akram," in *Iqra wa Rabukal Akhram* (Damascus, 1988), retrieved from http://www.jawdatsaid.net, translated by Halverson.
37. Qur'an 29:20, translated by Halverson.
38. See Halverson, *Theology and Creed.*
39. See Muslim Brotherhood, http://www.ikhwanweb.com/article.php?ID=15795 &SectionID=78.

Chapter 6: The Martyr

1. Mohamed A. Mahmoud, *Quest for Divinity: A Critical Examination of the Thought of Mahmud Mohammad Taha* (Syracuse, NY: Syracuse University Press, 2007), 12.
2. Gabriel Warburg, *Islam, Sectarianism, and Politics in Sudan since the Mahdiyya* (Madison: University of Wisconsin Press, 2002), 161.
3. Mahmoud, *Quest for Divinity*, 14.
4. Ibid., 16.
5. George Packer, "The Moderate Martyr: A Radically Peaceful Vision of Islam," *New Yorker* (September 11, 2006), http://www.newyorker.com/archive/2006/09/11 /060911fa_fact1.
6. This fact is one of the reasons the Sudanese-American scholar, Abdullahi A. Gallab, has characterized Mahmoud Taha as an "Islamist" in his book *The First Islamist Republic: Development and Disintegration of Islamism in Sudan* (London: Ashgate, 2008).
7. Packer, "The Moderate Martyr."
8. Ibid.
9. "The Emergence of a New Concept," The Republican Thought, http://www.alfikra .org/index_e.php.
10. Mahmoud, *Quest for Divinity*, 53–54.
11. Ibid.
12. Robert O. Collins, *A History of Modern Sudan* (Cambridge: Cambridge University Press, 2008), 72.
13. "Emergence of a New Concept."
14. "Questions from Mr. John Voll and Answers from Ustaz Mahmoud Mohammed Taha," The Republican Thought (July 17, 1963), http://www.alfikra.org/talk_page _view_e.php?talk_id=7&page_id=1.
15. Ibid., 2.
16. Ibid.
17. Mahmoud, *Quest for Divinity*, 20.
18. Ibid., 21.

19. Ibid.
20. Mahmoud Muhammad Taha, *The Second Message of Islam*, trans. Abdullahi Ahmed an-Na'im (Syracuse, NY: Syracuse University Press, 1987), 133.
21. Ibid., 137.
22. Ibid., 133–34.
23. Ibid., 166–67.
24. Mahmoud, *Quest for Divinity,* 22. See also "Emergence of a New Concept."
25. Quoted in Packer, "The Moderate Martyr."
26. Mahmoud, *Quest for Divinity*, 23.
27. "Emergence of a New Concept."
28. Abdullahi Ahmed an-Naim, "Translator's Introduction," in Taha, *Second Message*, 6–7.
29. Mahmoud, *Quest for Divinity*, 25.
30. Packer, "The Moderate Martyr."
31. Mahmoud, *Quest for Divinity,* 25.
32. Ibid., 26.
33. "Either This or the Flood," The Republican Thought (December 25, 1984), http://www.alfikra.org/article_page_ view_e.php?article_id=1001&page_id=1.
34. Ibid.
35. Mahmoud, *Quest for Divinity*, 27.
36. Ibid., 28.
37. An-Naim, "Translator's Introduction," 13.
38. "Ustazh Mahmoud's Statement before the Mockery Court of Mahallawy on January 7th, 1985," The Republican Thought (1985), http://www.alfikra.org/article_page_view_e.php?article_id=1002&page_id=1.
39. Mahmoud, *Quest for Divinity*, 28.
40. Ibid., 29.
41. Judith Miller, *God Has Ninety-Nine Names* (New York: Simon & Schuster, 1996), 12.
42. Mahmoud, *Quest for Divinity,* 30.
43. Declan O'Sullivan, "The Death Sentence for Mahmoud Muhammad Taha: Misuse of the Sudanese Legal System and Islamic Sharia Law?" *The International Journal of Human Rights* 5, no. 3 (Autumn 2001): 45–70.
44. Quoted in Packer, "The Moderate Martyr."
45. An-Naim, "Translator's Introduction," 1.
46. Abdullahi Ahmad an-Naim, *Toward an Islamic Reformation: Civil Liberties, Human Rights, and International Law* (Syracuse, NY: Syracuse University Press, 1990).

Chapter 7: The Cleric

1. "Brief Biography of: Grand Ayatollah Imam Muhammad Shirazi," Teachings of Islam, http://imamshirazi. com/imamshirazi.html.
2. Muhammad Mahdi al-Shirazi, *War, Peace, and Nonviolence: An Islamic Perspective*, trans. Ali ibn Adam and Z. Olyabek (London: Fountain Books, 2003), 116.
3. Laurence Louër, *Transnational Shia Politics: Religious and Political Networks in the Gulf* (New York: Columbia University Press, 2008), 101.
4. Abdelmalik Badruddin Eagle, "Translator's Note," in Muhammad Mahdi al-Shirazi, *What Is Islam? Beliefs, Principles, and a Way of Life* (London: Fountain

Books, 2002), http://www.alhassanain.com/english/book/book/beliefs_library
/religions_and_sects/what_is_islam_beliefs_principles_and_a_way_of_life/001.html.
5. Abdulaziz A. Sachedina, *The Just Ruler in Shi'ite Islam: The Comprehensive Authority of the Jurist in Imamite Jurisprudence* (New York: Oxford University Press, 1998), 23.
6. Eagle, "Translator's Note."
7. Al-Shirazi, *War, Peace, and Nonviolence*, 101.
8. Ibid., 103–4.
9. Ibid., 102.
10. Quoted in al-Shirazi, *War, Peace, and Nonviolence*, 105.
11. Al-Shirazi, *War, Peace, and Nonviolence*, 114.
12. Ibid., 116.
13. Ibid.
14. Ibid., 115.
15. Ibid., 104.
16. Ibid.
17. Ibid., 115.
18. Ibid., 13.
19. Ibid., 16.
20. Ibid., 118.
21. Ibid., 119.
22. Qur'an 41:34; trans. by Yusuf Ali and edited by Halverson.
23. Al-Shirazi, *War, Peace, and Nonviolence,* 122.
24. Quoted in ibid., 123.
25. Ibid., 127.
26. Quoted ibid., 124.
27. Ibid., 125.
28. Hassan Qazwini, *American Crescent* (New York: Random House, 2007), 4.
29. Charles Tripp, *A History of Iraq* (New York: Cambridge University Press, 2007), 203.
30. Nikki R. Keddie, *Modern Iran: Roots and Results of Revolution,* updated ed. (New Haven, CT: Yale University Press, 2006), 240.
31. Ibid., 241.
32. Louër, *Transnational Shia Politics*, 188.
33. Ibid., 194.
34. Muhammad G. Ayub, *Aspects of the Political Theory of Imam Muhammad Shirazi*, 2nd ed. (London: Fountain Books, 2004), 18–19.
35. Quoted in ibid., 21.
36. Ibid., 21–22.
37. Ibid., 33.
38. Quoted in ibid., 34.
39. Quoted in ibid., 38.
40. Quoted in ibid., 39.
41. Qur'an 2:173, trans. by Yusuf Ali and edited by Halverson.
42. Ayub, *Aspects of the Political Theory,* 40.
43. Ibid., 42.
44. Azadeh Moaveni, "Invasion of the Corpse Snatchers," *Time* (Dec. 21, 2001), http://www.time.com/time/magazine/article/0,9171,189483,00.html.

45. Ibid.
46. Muhammad Khurasani, "Iran Authorities Hold Late Marjay Ash-Shirazi's Sons and Women," Jafariya News (August 11, 2005), http://www.jafariyanews.com /2k5_news/aug/11 shirazifamily_arrested.htm.
47. Louër, *Transnational Shia Politics*, 195.
48. Ibid., 92.
49. Ibid., 95–96.
50. Ibid., 93.
51. "Abstract of the Speech Given by Eminent Marja Ayatollah al-Udhma Sayyid Sadiq Shirazi on the Day after the Funeral of the Late Ayatollah al-Udhma al-Imam Sayyid Muhammad Shirazi," MyInfo UK, www.myinfo.ukonline.co.uk/sadiq speech.htm (no longer available).

Chapter 8: The Ascetic
1. Sunil Shukla, "Maulana Wahiduddin Khan: Recipient of Rajiv Gandhi National Sadbhavana Award," Broadcasting Corporation of India (no date), http://news onair.com/Maulana-Wahiduddin-Khan-Recipient-of-Rajiv-Gandhi-National -Sadbhavana-Award.asp.
2. "Maulana Wahiduddin Khan," Al-Risala Forum International (no date), http:// www.alrisala.org/intro_page_links/maulana_wahiduddin_khan.htm.
3. Ibid.; Yoginder Sikand, "Analysis of the Writings of Maulana Wahidudduin Khan-i," *The Milli Gazette* (March 1, 2002), http://www.milligazette.com/Archives /01032002/0103200280.htm.
4. Sikand, "Analysis of the Writings."
5. Sayyed Vali Reza Nasr, *Mawdudi and the Making of Islamic Revivalism* (New York: Oxford University Press, 1996), 41.
6. Ibid., 110.
7. Ibid.
8. Wahiduddin Khan, *God Arises*, trans. Farida Khanam (New Delhi: Goodword Books, 2001), 8.
9. Ibid., 9.
10. Ibid., 200.
11. Irfan A. Omar, "Islam and the Other: The Ideal Vision of Mawlana Wahiduddin Khan," *Journal of Ecumenical Studies* 36, no. 3/4 (1999): 423–38.
12. Sikand, "Analysis of the Writings."
13. Jan Ali, "Islamic Revivalism: The Case of the Tablighi Jamaat," *Journal of Muslim Minority Affairs* 23, no.1 (2003): 175.
14. Sikand, "Analysis of the Writings."
15. Wahiduddin Khan, *Islam and Peace*, trans. Farida Khanam (New Delhi: Goodword Books, 2003), 98.
16. Ibid., 99–100.
17. Ibid., 100.
18. Ibid., 169.
19. Ibid., 170.
20. Ibid., 171.
21. Ibid.

22. Daniel C. Peterson, *Muhammad: Prophet of God* (Grand Rapids, MI: Eerdmans, 2007), 130–33.
23. Ibid., 133.
24. Khan, *Islam and Peace*, 121.
25. Ibid., 173.
26. Peterson, *Muhammad*, 135.
27. Ibid., 134.
28. Khan, *Islam and Peace*, 119.
29. Ibid., 123.
30. Ibid.
31. Ibid., 120.
32. "Timeline: Ayodhya Mosque Crisis," BBC News (November, 23, 2009), http://news.bbc.co.uk/2/hi/ south_asia/1844930.stm.
33. Akbar S. Ahmed, *Jinnah, Pakistan and Islamic Identity: The Search for Saladin* (New York: Routledge, 1997), 243.
34. Wahiduddin Khan, "Ayodhya's Sole Solution," *al-Risala* (January–February 1993): 4.
35. Ibid., 9–11.
36. Harihar Swarup, "Islam Doesn't Preach Violence, Says Wahiduddin Khan," *The Tribune* (September 5, 2010), http://www.tribuneindia.com/2010/20100905/edit.htm#4.
37. Khan, "Ayodhya's Sole Solution," 3.
38. Ibid., 10.
39. Khan, *Islam and Peace*, 100.
40. Yoginder Sikand, "Analysis of the Writings of Maulana Wahiduddin Khan—II," *Milli Gazette* (March 15, 2002), http://www.milligazette.com/Archives/15032002/1503200247.htm.
41. See, e.g., Ornit Shani, *Communalism, Cast and Hindu Nationalism: The Violence in Gujarat* (New York: Cambridge University Press, 2007).
42. Sikand, "Analysis of the Writings of Maulana Wahiduddin Khan—II."
43. "Maulana Wahiduddin Khan Receives Demiurgus Peace Award," *Milli Gazette* (November 1, 2002), http://www.milligazette.com/Archives/01112002/0111200266.htm.
44. "About Us," CPS International, http://www.cpsglobal.or g/content/about-us.
45. "Islam: A Religion of Peace," CPS International, http://cpsglobal.org/content/islam-religion-peace.

Chapter 9: Microfinance
1. Stephen Foly, "What Financial Crisis? Number of Billionaires Hits New High?" *The Independent* (March 11, 2010), http://www.independent.co.uk/news/people/news/what-financial-crisis-number-of-billionaires-hits-new-high-1919449.html.
2. "Monthly Budget Review: Fiscal Year 2009: A Congressional Budget Office Analysis," Congressional Budget Office, (October 7, 2009) http://www.cbo.gov/ftpdocs/106xx/doc10640/10-2009-MBR.pdf.
3. "First Loan He Gave Was $27 from Own Pocket," *Daily Star* online, vol. 5, no. 849 (October 14, 2006), http://www.thedailystar.net/2006/10/14/d6101401033.htm.

4. "Biography of Dr. Muhammad Yunus," Grameen Bank, http://www.grameen-info
.org/index.php?option=com_content&task=view&id=329&Itemid=363.
5. "About Professor Yunus: Education," Yunus Centre, http://www.muhammad
yunus.org/ About-Professor-Yunus/about-professor-yunus-education/.
6. "Bangladesh Sets Up War Crimes Court," Al-Jazeera (March 25, 2010), http://
english.aljazeera.net/news/asia/2010/03/2010325151839747356.html.
7. Kaushik Basu and Ravi Kanbur, *Arguments for a Better World: Essays in Honor
of Amartya Sen; Volume II—Society, Institutions, and Development* (New York:
Oxford University Press, 2009), 221.
8. Muhammad Yunus, *Building Social Business: The New Kind of Capitalism That
Serves Humanity's Most Pressing Needs* (New York: Public Affairs, 2010), viii.
9. Ibid.
10. Qur'an 2:278, trans. by Halverson.
11. Sahih Bukhari, vol. 2, no. 468, University of Southern California, http://www.usc
.edu/schools/college/crcc/engagement/resources/texts/muslim/hadith
/bukhari/023.sbt.html.
12. Sunan Abu Dawud, book 22, no. 3327, University of Southern California, http://
www.usc.edu/schools/college/crcc/engagement/resources/texts/muslim/hadith
/abudawud/022.sat.html.
13. Carolyn Fluehr-Lobban, *Islamic Society in Practice* (Gainesville: University Press
of Florida, 1994), 165–66.
14. Nimrah Karim, Michael Tarazi, and Xavier Reille, "Islamic Microfinance: An
Emerging Market Niche," *Focus Note*, no. 49 (August 2008): 1.
15. Ibid., 166.
16. Mahmoud A. El-Gamal, *Islamic Finance: Law, Economics, and Finance* (Cambridge: Cambridge University Press, 2002), 120.
17. Ibid., 121.
18. Fluehr-Lobban, *Islamic Society in Practice*, 166.
19. El-Gamal, *Islamic Finance*, 13.
20. Ibid., 14.
21. Ibid., 18.
22. Yunus, *Building Social Business,* ix.
23. Ibid.
24. Charles Wankel, *Alleviating Poverty through Business Strategy* (New York: Palgrave
Macmillan, 2008), 149.
25. Yunus, *Building Social Business,* x.
26. Ibid.
27. Ibid., xiii.
28. Anand Giridharadas and Keith Bradsher, "Microloan Pioneer and His Bank Win
Nobel Peace Prize," *New York Times* (October 13, 2006), http://www.nytimes
.com/2006/10/13/business/14nobelcnd.html?_r=1&scp=2&sq=1974%20famine
%20bangladesh&st=cse.
29. Muhammad Yunus and Alan Jolis, *Banker to the Poor: Micro-Lending and the
Battle Against World Poverty* (New York: Public Affairs, 2003), 110.
30. "Usurers up in Arms to Usurp Politics, Hasina Tells Cultural Activists," BDNews24
.com (February 17, 2007), http://64.150.182.63/details.php?id=52308&cid=3.

31. See, e.g., Jonathan J. Morduch, "The Microfinance Promise," *Journal of Economic Literature* 37 (December 1999): 1569–1614.
32. Mark Engler, "The Godfather of Microcredit: Muhammad Yunus' Vision of 'Social Business' Is a Curious Amalgam of Left and Right," *The Indypendent* (February 19, 2007), http://www.indypendent.org/ 2010/02/18/godfather-of-microcredit/.
33. See http://www.grameenphone.com/index.php?id=68.
34. "Grameen Heritage," Grameen Foundation, http://www.grameenfoundation.org /who-we-are/grameen-heritage.
35. "Grameen Jameel Pan Arab Microfinance Ltd.," Grameen Foundation, http:// www.grameenfoundation.org/what-we-do/initiatives/grameen-jameel-pan-arab -microfinance-ltd.
36. "Home," Grameen-Jameel, http://www.grameen-jameel.com/.
37. "Zeinab, Egypt," Grameen Foundation, http://www.grameenfoundation.org/our -impact/zeinab-egypt.
38. "What Is Microfinance? What Is Village Banking?" FINCA, http://www.finca.org /site/c.6fIGIXMFJnJ0H/b.6088437/k.FEF1/What_is_Microfinance_What_is_ Village_Banking.htm.
39. Melissa Duscha, "Microcapital Story: Islamic Microfinance Rapidly Growing in Afghanistan," MicroCapital (February 27, 2008), http://www.microcapital.org /microcapital-story-islamic-microfinance-rapidly-growing-in-afghanistan/.
40. FINCA, http://www.finca.org/site/c.6fIGIXMFJnJ0H/b.6088547/k.87E1 /Afghanistan.htm.
41. Global Security, http://www.globalsecurity.org/military/library/budget/fy1999 /dote/army/99m1a2.html.
42. "Jordan," FINCA, http://www.finca.org/site/c.6fIGIXMFJnJ0H/b.6088607/k.C484 /Jordan.htm.
43. "About Us," FINCA Jordan, http://www.finca-jordan.org/About%20Us.htm.
44. FINCA, http://www.finca.org/site/c.6fIGIXMFJnJ0H/b.6088607/k.C484/Jordan .htm.
45. "Queen Highlights Power of Microfinance, Tours FINCA Jordan Microbusi-nesses," *Jordan Times* (February 26, 2008), http://www.jordantimes.com/?news =5963&searchFor=FINCA %20Jordan.
46. "King Abdullah II," King Abdullah, http://www.kingabdullah.jo/main.php?main _page =0&lang_hmka1=1.
47. "The First MicroFinanceBank Ltd and Pakistan Post Office Agree to Expand Mi-crofinance Services for the Poor," Aga Khan Development Network (January 28, 2010), from http://www.akdn.org/Content/961.
48. "Microfinance in Tajikistan," Aga Khan Agency for Microfinance, http://www .akdn.org/ akam_tajikistan.asp.
49. "Microfinance in Egypt," Aga Khan Agency for Microfinance, http://www.akdn .org/aka m_egypt.asp.
50. Beatriz Armendariz and Jonathan Morduch, *The Economics of Microfinance*, 2nd ed. (Cambridge, MA: MIT Press, 2010), x.
51. Karim, Tarazi, and Reille, "Islamic Microfinance," 13.
52. Ibid.
53. Dwight David Eisenhower, "The Chance for Peace," speech given to the American Society of Newspaper Editors, April 16, 1953.

Chapter 10: Women's Education

1. Cited and translated from the *Nahj al-Fasahah* by Husayn Naghavi, "Pearls of Wisdom: A Selection of Hadiths from the Prophet Muhammad," *Message of Thaqalayn* 10, no. 3 (Autumn 2009): 131.
2. This prophetic tradition, like the preceding one, circulates widely in contemporary Muslim oral tradition. It is recorded in Al-Majlisi's *Bihar al-Anwar* and a variant is also recorded in *Sunan Ibn Majah* as hadith number 224.
3. See, e.g., Aaron Benavot, "Education, Gender, and Economic Development: A Cross-National Study," *Sociology of Education* 62, no. 1 (January 1989): 14–32; Josh Gibson, "Can Women's Education Aid Economic Development? The Effect on Child Stunting in Papua New Guinea," *Pacific Economic Bulletin* 14 (1999): 71–81; Farzaneh Roudi-Fahimi and Valentine M. Moghadam, *Empowering Women, Developing Society: Female Education in the Middle East and North Africa* (Washington, DC: Population Reference Bureau, 2003).
4. Caren Grown, Geeta Rao Gupta, and Asilihan Kes, *Education and Gender Equality, Taking Action: Achieving Gender Equality and Empowering Women* (London: Earthscan, 2005), 47.
5. Ibid., 45.
6. "Afghanistan," *The CIA World Fact Book* (Washington, DC: Central Intelligence Agency, 2010).
7. "Jordan," ibid.
8. "Somalia," ibid.
9. "Egypt," ibid.
10. Leila Ahmed, *Women and Gender in Islam* (New Haven, CT: Yale University Press, 1992), 60.
11. Matthew S. Gordon, *The Rise of Islam* (Indianapolis, IN: Hackett, 2005), 104.
12. Muhammad Zubayr Siddiqi, *Hadith Literature: Its Origin, Development, and Special Features* (Cambridge, UK: Islamic Texts Society, 1993), 118.
13. Ibid., 119.
14. Valerie J. Hoffman, "Muslim Sainthood, Women, and the Legend of Sayyida Nafisa," in *Women Saints in World Religions*, ed. Arvind Sharma (Albany: SUNY Press, 2000), 124.
15. Ibid., 126.
16. Imam Metawalli ash-Sharawi, "Nafisa at-Tahira," an excerpt from *From the Light of Ahl al-Bayt: My Spiritual Experiences Unveiled*, As Sunnah Foundation of America, http://www.sunnah.org/history/Scholars/nafisa_at_tahira.htm.
17. Y. G. M. Lulat, *A History of African Higher Education from Antiquity to the Present: A Critical Synthesis* (Westport, CT: Praeger, 2005), 70.
18. "Al-Qarawiyyin Mosque and University," Muslim Heritage (October 2004), http://www.muslimheritage.com/topics/default.cfm?ArticleID=447.
19. James E. Lindsay, *Daily Life in the Medieval Islamic World* (Indianapolis, IN: Hackett, 2008), 198.
20. Fatima Mernissi, *Forgotten Queens of Islam* (Minneapolis: University of Minnesota Press, 1993), 115; J. A. Boyle, ed. *The Cambridge History of Iran, Volume 5: The Saljuq and Mongo Periods* (Cambridge: Cambridge University Press, 1968), 216.
21. Ahmed, *Women and Gender in Islam*, 114.

22. Carla Power, "A Secret History," *New York Times* (February 25, 2007), http://www.nytimes.com/2007/02/25/magazine/25wwlnEssay.t.html.
23. Jehangir Pocha, "Rebiya Kadeer: Uighur Dalai Lama," *In These Times* 30, no. 12 (December 2006): 36.
24. "Rebiya Kadeer," *New York Times* (July 30, 2009), http://topics.nytimes.com/ top/reference/timestopics/people/k/rebiya_kadeer/index.html?scp=1 -spot&sq=rebiya kadeer&st=cse.
25. Robert Marquand, "Q & A with Uighur Spiritual Leader Rebiya Kadeer," *Christian Science Monitor* (July 12, 2009): 6.
26. Quoted in Easwaran, *Man to Match His Mountains*, 168.
27. Michel Hoebink, "Mahmoud Taha: The Gandhi of Sudan," Radio Netherlands (January 1, 2006), http://static.rnw.nl/migratie/www.radionetherlands.nl/current affairs/region/africa/sud060118-redirected.
28. Wahiduddin Khan, "Woman's Role in Islam," CPS International, http://www.cpsglobal.o rg/content/woman%E2%80%99s-role-islam-0.
29. Quoted in Daisy Khan, "Time for a Women's Jihad against Violence," *Washington Post* (July 22, 2009), http://newsweek.washingtonpost.com/onfaith/panelists /daisy_khan/2009/07/time_for_a_ womens_jihad_against_violence.html.
30. Muhammad al-Shirazi, "On the Status of Women in Islam," excerpted from *Islamic Government* (no date), 104–123, Teachings of Islam, http://imamshirazi.com /womanstatus.html.
31. Caren Grown, Geeta Rao Gupta, and Asilihan Kes, *Education and Gender Equality, Taking Action: Achieving Gender Equality and Empowering Women* (London: Earthscan, 2005), 47–48.
32. Ibid.
33. Ibid.
34. Ibid., 48–49.
35. Ibid., 49.
36. Ibid.
37. Simeen Mahmud and Sajeda Amin, "Girls' Schooling and Marriage in Rural Bangladesh," in *Children's Lives and Schooling Across Societies*, eds. Emily Hannum and Bruce Fuller (Oxford: JAI Press, 2006), 71.
38. Emily Hannum and Bruce Fuller, "Overview: Children's Lives and Schooling across Societies," in *Children's Lives*, eds. Hannum and Fuller, 6.
39. Queen Rania, http://www.queenrania.jo/media/press/queen-rania-speaks-innovative -financing-education-conference.
40. Ibid., 50.
41. Alissa Shapiro, "Rural Egypt," UNICEF (August 19, 2010), http://www.unicef usa.org/ news/ news-from-the-field/education-reaches-girls-in-rural-egypt.html.
42. Ibid.
43. Grown, Gupta, and Kes, *Education and Gender Equality*," 51.
44. Ibid.
45. Ibid.
46. Cecilia Sem Obeng, "Poverty and Early Marriage as a Hindrance to Rural Girls' Schooling,"*Progress in Education,* vol. 11 (Huntington, NY: Nova Science Publishers, 2003), 146.

47. Grown, Gupta, and Kes, *"Education and Gender Equality,"* 51.

48. Ibid.

Chapter 11: Jihad without Swords

1. Qur'an 9:20, trans. by Halverson.

2. Sunan Abu Dawud, book 14, no. 2505, University of Southern California, http://www.usc.edu/schools/college/crcc/engagement/resources/texts/muslim/hadith/abudawud/014.sat.html.

3. Sahih Bukhari, vol. 4, book 52, no. 248, University of Southern California,http://www.usc.edu/schools/college/crcc/engagement/resources/texts/muslim/hadith/bukhari/052.sbt.html#004.052.248.

4. Sahih Bukhari, vol. 3, book 29, no. 84, University of Southern California,http://www.usc.edu/schools/college/crcc/engagement/resources/texts/muslim/hadith/bukhari/029.sbt.html#003.029.084.

5. See "by plague": al-Muwatta 8.2.6, 16.12.36, Bukhari 7.71.629, Abu Dawud 20.3105; "by disease of the stomach": al-Muwatta 8.2.6, 16.12.36, Bukhari 7.71.629; "by drowning": al-Muwatta 8.2.6, 16.12.36; "by collapsing building": al-Muwatta 8.2.6, 16.12.36, Abu Dawud 20.3105; "by fire": al-Muwatta 16.12.36, Abu Dawud 20.3105; "by childbirth": al-Muwatta 16.12.36, Abu Dawud 20.3105; "by protecting property": Bukhari 3.43.660, Muslim 1.0260; "by falling from horse or camel": Abu Dawud 14.2493; "by sting of poison creature": Abu Dawud 14.2493; "by defending family": Abu Dawud 40.4754.

6. Martin Lings, *Muhammad: His Life Based on the Earliest Sources* (Cambridge: Islamic Texts Society, 1991), 79–80.

7. Qur'an 3:157, translated by Abullah Yusuf Ali.

8. Felicitas Meta Maria Opwis, *Maslaha and the Purpose of the Law: Islamic Discourse on Legal Change from the 4th/10th to 8th/14th Century* (Leiden: Brill, 2010), 2.

9. Joseph Schacht, "Muhammad Abduh," in *E. J. Brill's First Encyclopedia of Islam: 1913–1936*, eds. M. T. Houtsma, A. J. Wensinck, and T. W. Arnold (Leiden, Netherlands: Brill, 1993), 679.

10. "Countries: Afghanistan," Word Food Programme (2010), http://www.wfp.org/countries/afghanistan.

11. Mohammed Abu-Nimer, *Nonviolence and Peace Building in Islam: Theory and Practice* (Gainesville, FL: University of Florida Press, 2003), 3.

12. Ibid., 166–67.

13. Ibid., 167.

14. Mark Sorkin, "Letter from Budrus," *The Nation* (June 14, 2004), http://www.thenation. com/article/letter-budrus.

15. Nicholas D. Kristof, "Waiting for Gandhi," *New York Times* (July 10, 2010), http://www.nytimes.com/2010/07/11/opinion/11kristof.html?src=me&scp=9&sq=budrus&st=cse.

16. Saeed Kamali Dehghan and Matthew Taylor, "Neda Agha-Soltan: 'She Is Dead but Regime Is Still Afraid of Her," *The Guardian* (June 11, 2010), http://www.guardian.co.uk/world/2010/jun /11/neda-agha-soltan-iran-killing.

17. Nazila Fathi, "In a Death Seen around the World, a Symbol of Iranian Protests," *New York Times* (June 23, 2009), http://www.nytimes.com/2009/06/23/world/middleeast/23neda.html.

18. Ibid.
19. "Neda's Mother Appeals for Help in Finding Killer," CNN (August 30, 2010), http://www.cnn.com/2010/WORLD/meast/08/30/iran.neda.mother/index.html ? hpt=T2.
20. Brian Ross and Matthew Cole, "Egypt: The Face That Launched a Revolution," ABC News (February 4, 2011), http://abcnews.go.com/Blotter/egypt-face-launched -revolution/story?id=12841488&page=1.
21. Steven R. Corman and Jill Schiefelbein, *Communication and Media Strategy in the Jihadi War of Ideas* (Tempe, AZ: Consortium for Strategic Communication, 2006).
22. Martin Luther King Jr., "The American Dream," ed. James M. Washington, *A Testament of Hope: The Essential Writings and Speeches of Martin Luther King Jr.* (New York: HarperCollins, 1986), 215.

SELECTED BIBLIOGRAPHY

Abu-Nimer, Mohammed. *Nonviolence and Peace Building in Islam: Theory and Practice*. Gainesville: University Press of Florida, 2003.

Agrawal, Lion M. G. *Freedom Fighters of India*. Delhi, India: Isha Books, 2008.

Ahmad, Aisha, and Roger Boase. *Pashtun Tales from the Pakistan-Afghan Frontier*. London: Saqi Books, 2003.

Ahmed, Akbar S. *Jinnah, Pakistan and Islamic Identity: The Search for Saladin*. New York: Routledge, 1997.

Ahmed, Leila. *Women and Gender in Islam*. New Haven, CT: Yale University Press, 1992.

Arendt, Hannah. *On Violence*. New York: Harcourt, Brace & World, 1970.

Arkoun, Mohammad. *The Unthought in Contemporary Islamic Thought*. London: Saqi Books, 2002.

Armendariz, Beatriz, and Jonathan Morduch. *The Economics of Microfinance*. 2nd ed. Cambridge, MA: MIT Press, 2010.

Aust, Anthony. *Handbook of International Law*. 2nd ed. New York: Cambridge University Press, 2010.

Ayub, Muhammad G. *Aspects of the Political Theory of Imam Muhammad Shirazi*. 2nd ed. London: Fountain Books, 2004.

Basu, Kaushik, and Ravi Kanbur. *Arguments for a Better World: Essays in Honor of Amartya Sen; Volume II—Society, Institutions, and Development*. New York: Oxford University Press, 2009.

Binder, Leonard. *Islamic Liberalism: A Critique of Development Ideologies*. Chicago: University of Chicago Press, 1988.

Boyle, J. A., ed. *The Cambridge History of Iran, Volume 5: The Saljuq and Mongo Periods*. Cambridge: Cambridge University Press, 1968.

Burritt, Elihu, and Charles Northend. *Elihu Burritt: A Memorial Volume Containing a Sketch of His Life and Labors*. New York: D. Appleton, 1880.

Casanova, José. *Public Religions in the Modern World*. Chicago: University of Chicago Press, 1994.

Chomsky, Noam. *9-11*. New York: Seven Stories, 2001.

Cohen, Robert, and Reginald E. Zelnik, eds. *The Free Speech Movement: Reflections on Berkeley in the 1960s*. Berkeley: University of California Press, 2002.

Collins, Robert O. *A History of Modern Sudan*. Cambridge: Cambridge University Press, 2008.

Easwaran, Eknath. *A Man to Match Mountains: Badshah Khan, Nonviolent Soldier of Islam*. Berkeley, CA: Nilgiri, 1984.

———. *Nonviolent Soldier of Islam*. Tomales, CA: Nilgiri, 2002.

El-Gamal, Mahmoud A. *Islamic Finance: Law, Economics, and Finance*. Cambridge: Cambridge University Press, 2002.

Enzensberger, Hans Magnus. *Civil Wars: From L.A. to Bosnia*. New York: New Press, 1993.

Finkelman, Paul, ed. *Encyclopedia of African American History 1896 to the Present*. New York: Oxford University Press, 2009.

Fluehr-Lobban, Carolyn. *Islamic Society in Practice*. Gainesville: University Press of Florida, 1994.

Gallab, Abdullahi A. *The First Islamist Republic: Development and Disintegration of Islamism in Sudan*. London: Ashgate, 2008.

Garrow, David J. *Bearing the Cross: Martin Luther King Jr. and the Southern Christian Leadership Conference*. New York: HarperCollins, 1986.

Gordon, Matthew S. *The Rise of Islam*. Indianapolis, IN: Hackett, 2005.

Gottschall, Jonathan, and David Sloan Wilson, eds. *The Literary Animal: Evolution and the Nature of Narrative*. Chicago: Northwestern University Press, 2005.

Grown, Caren, Geeta Rao Gupta, and Asilihan Kes. *Education and Gender Equality, Taking Action: Achieving Gender Equality and Empowering Women*. London: Earthscan, 2005.

Halverson, Jeffry R. *Theology and Creed in Sunni Islam: The Muslim Brotherhood, Ash'arism, and Political Sunnism*. New York: Palgrave Macmillan, 2010.

Halverson, Jeffry R., H. L. Goodall Jr., and Steven R. Corman. *Master Narratives of Islamist Extremism*. New York: Palgrave Macmillan, 2011.

Hammond, Andrew. *Popular Culture in the Arab World: Arts, Politics, and Media*. New York: American University in Cairo Press, 2007.

Hannum, Emily, and Bruce Fuller, eds. *Children's Lives and Schooling across Societies*. Oxford: JAI Press, 2006.

Haroon, Sana. *Frontier of Faith: Islam in the Indo-Afghan Borderland*. New York: Columbia University Press, 2007.

Hastings, Tom H. *The Lessons of Nonviolence: Theory and Practice in a World of Conflict*. Jefferson, NC: McFarland, 2006.

Hirschon, Renée, ed. *Crossing the Aegean: An Appraisal of the 1923 Compulsory Population Exchange between Greece and Turkey*. New York: Berghahn Books, 2003.

Houtsma, M. T., A. J. Wensinck, and T. W. Arnold, eds. *E. J. Brill's First Encyclopedia of Islam: 1913–1936*. Leiden, Netherlands: Brill, 1993.

Iqbal, Muhammad. *The Reconstruction of Islamic Thought*. Gloucestershire, UK: Dodo, 2009.

Jones, Seth G. *Counterinsurgency in Afghanistan*. Washington: Rand Corporation, 2008.

Keddie, Nikki R. *Modern Iran: Roots and Results of Revolution*. Updated ed. New Haven, CT: Yale University Press, 2006.

Khan, Abdul Ghaffar (Badshah Khan). *My Life and Struggle*. Translated by Helen H. Bouman. Delhi: Hind Pocket Books, 1969.

Khan, Wahiduddin. *God Arises*. Translated by Farida Khanam. New Delhi: Goodword Books, 2001.

———. *Islam and Peace*. Translated by Farida Khanam. New Delhi: Goodword Books, 2003.

King, Martin Luther, Jr. *The Autobiography of Martin Luther King Jr.* Edited by Clayborne Carson. New York: Grand Central, 2001.

Lincoln, Bruce. *Holy Terrors: Thinking about Religion after September 11*. Chicago: University of Chicago Press, 2005.

Lindsay, James E. *Daily Life in the Medieval Islamic World*. Indianapolis, IN: Hackett, 2008.

Lings, Martin. *Muhammad: His Life Based on the Earliest Sources*. Cambridge: Islamic Texts Society, 1991.

Louër, Laurence. *Transnational Shia Politics: Religious and Political Networks in the Gulf*. New York: Columbia University Press, 2008.

Lulat, Y. G. M. *A History of African Higher Education from Antiquity to the Present: A Critical Synthesis*. Westport, CT: Praeger, 2005.

Mahmoud, Mohamed A. *Quest for Divinity: A Critical Examination of the Thought of Mahmud Mohammad Taha*. Syracuse, NY: Syracuse University Press, 2007.

Mayton, Daniel M. *Nonviolence and Peace Psychology: Intrapersonal, Interpersonal, Societal, and World Peace*. New York: Springer, 2009.

Mernissi, Fatima. *Forgotten Queens of Islam*. Minneapolis: University of Minnesota Press, 1993.

Millar, James R., ed. *Encyclopedia of Russian History, Vol. 4*. New York: Macmillan Reference USA, 2004.

Miller, Judith. *God Has Ninety-Nine Names*. New York: Simon & Schuster, 1996.

Minault, Gail. *The Khilafat Movement: Religious Symbolism and Political Mobilization in India*. New York: Columbia University Press, 1982.

Münkler, Herfried. *Empires: The Logic of World Domination from Ancient Rome to the United States*. Translated by Patrick Camiller. Malden, MA: Polity Press, 2007.

An-Naim, Abdullahi Ahmad. *Toward an Islamic Reformation: Civil Liberties, Human Rights, and International Law*. Syracuse, NY: Syracuse University Press, 1990.

Nasr, Sayyed Vali Reza. *Mawdudi and the Making of Islamic Revivalism*. New York: Oxford University Press, 1996.

Nata, R., ed. *Progress in Education, Volume 11*. Huntington, NY: Nova Science Publishers, 2003.

Nicolle, David, and Graham Turner. *Poitiers AD 732: Charles Martel Turns the Islamic Tide*. New York: Osprey, 2008.

Opwis, Felicitas Meta Maria. *Maslaha and the Purpose of the Law: Islamic Discourse on Legal Change from the 4th/10th to 8th/14th Century*. Leiden, Netherlands: Brill, 2010.

Peterson, Daniel C. *Muhammad: Prophet of God*. Grand Rapids, MI: Eerdmans, 2007.

Qazwini, Hassan. *American Crescent*. New York: Random House, 2007.

Qutb, Sayyid. *Milestones*. USA: SIME Journal, 2005.

Rushby, Kevin. *Children of Kali: Through India in Search of Bandits, the Thug Cult, and the British Raj*. New York: Walker, 2002.

Sachedina, Abdulaziz A. *The Just Ruler in Shi'ite Islam: The Comprehensive Authority of the Jurist in Imamite Jurisprudence*. New York: Oxford University Press, 1998.

Saeed, Jawdat. *The Doctrine of Adam's First Son*. Translated by Munzer A. Absi and H. Hilwani. Damascus: Dar al-Fikr, 1993.

————. *Hatta Yughayyiru Ma Bi-Anfusihim*. Damascus: Dar al-Fikr, 1972.

Scott, James C. *Seeing Like a State: How Certain Schemes to Improve the Human Condition Have Failed*. New Haven, CT: Yale University Press, 1998.

Sharma, Arvind, ed. *Women Saints in World Religions*. Albany, NY: SUNY Press, 2000.

Al-Shirazi, Muhammad Mahdi. *War, Peace, and Nonviolence: An Islamic Perspective*. Translated by Ali ibn Adam and Z. Olyabek. London: Fountain Books, 2003.

————. *What Is Islam? Beliefs, Principles, and a Way of Life*. London: Fountain Books, 2002.

Siddiqi, Muhammad Zubayr. *Hadith Literature: Its Origin, Development, and Special Features*. Cambridge: Islamic Texts Society, 1993.

Steger, Manfred B. *Judging Nonviolence: The Dispute between Realists and Idealists*. New York: Routledge, 2003.

Stout, Martha. *The Sociopath Next Door*. New York: Broadway, 2005.

Taha, Mahmoud Muhammad. *The Second Message of Islam*. Translated by Abdullahi Ahmed an-Naim. Syracuse, NY: Syracuse University Press, 1987.

Talbot, Ian. *Pakistan: A Modern History*. New York: Palgrave Macmillan, 1999.

Tamimi, Azzam S. *Rachid Ghannouchi: A Democrat within Islamism*. New York: Oxford University Press, 2001.

Tidrick, Kathryn. *Gandhi: A Political and Spiritual Life*. London: I. B. Tauris, 2006.

Tilly, Charles, ed. *The Formation of National States in Western Europe*. Princeton, NJ: Princeton University Press, 1975.

Tolstoy, Leo. *The Kingdom of God Is within You*. Translated by Constance Garnett. New York: Kessinger, 2004.

————. *Writings on Civil Disobedience and Nonviolence*. Philadelphia: New Society, 1987.

Tripp, Charles. *A History of Iraq*. New York: Cambridge University Press, 2007.

Wankel, Charles. *Alleviating Poverty through Business Strategy*. New York: Palgrave Macmillan, 2008.

Warburg, Gabriel. *Islam, Sectarianism, and Politics in Sudan since the Mahdiyya*. Madison: University of Wisconsin Press, 2002.

Washington, James Melvin, ed. *A Testament of Hope: The Essential Writings and Speeches of Martin Luther King Jr.*. New York: HarperCollins, 1986.

Wink, Walter, ed. *Peace Is the Way: Writings on Nonviolence from the Fellowship of Reconciliation*. New York: Orbis Books, 2000.

Wolpert, Stanley, ed. *Encyclopedia of India, Vol. 2*. Detroit: Charles Scribner's Sons, 2006.

Yunus, Muhammad. *Building Social Business: The New Kind of Capitalism That Serves Humanity's Most Pressing Needs*. New York: PublicAffairs, 2010.

Yunus, Muhammad, and Alan Jolis. *Banker to the Poor: Micro-Lending and the Battle against World Poverty*. New York: PublicAffairs, 2003.

Zalta, Edward N., ed. *The Stanford Encyclopedia of Philosophy*. Stanford, CA: Metaphysics Research Lab, 2005.

Al-Zayyat, Montasser. *The Road to al-Qaeda: The Story of Bin Laden's Right Hand Man*. Translated by Ahmed Fekhry. London: Pluto, 2004.

INDEX

velayat-e faqih, 97, 98. *See also* Khomeini,
   Ruhullah
Vietnam War, 33

West Bank, *see* Palestine
World War I, 7, 27, 51–52
World War II, 7, 12, 30, 62, 63. *See also*
   Nazi Germany

Yunus, Muhammad, 41, 112–13, 114–
   17, 130

Zakaria, Fareed, 16
zakat (alms), 20, 51, 52, 119
Zarqawi, Abu Musab al-, 22
Zawahiri, Ayman al-, 12–13, 14

ABOUT THE AUTHOR

Jeffry R. Halverson is an Islamic studies scholar and historian of religions, specializing in the Middle East and North Africa. He currently serves as assistant research professor in the Hugh Downs School of Human Communication at Arizona State University (Tempe). He received his BS from Nazareth College in Rochester, New York, studied Islam in Cairo as a Fulbright fellow, and received his MA and PhD in Islamic studies from the Department of Religious Studies at Arizona State University. He is the author of *Theology and Creed in Sunni Islam* (2010) and lead author of *Master Narratives of Islamist Extremism* (2011). Halverson's scholarship has also been published in several academic journals and reference works. He lives in Phoenix, Arizona.